MATT
TEBBUTT
COOKS
COUNTRY

MITCHELL BEAZLEY

PHOTOGRAPHS BY CHRIS TERRY

MATT TEBBUTT

COOKS COUNTRY

MODERN RURAL BRITISH FOOD

For Lisa, Jessie and Henry, without whom no meal is ever complete.

Matt Tebbutt Cooks Country

First published in Great Britain in 2008 by
Mitchell Beazley, an imprint of Octopus
Publishing Group Limited,
2–4 Heron Quays, London E14 4JP.
An Hachette Livre UK Company

© Octopus Publishing Group Limited 2008
Text © Matt Tebbutt 2008
Photographs © Chris Terry 2008

A CIP catalogue record for this book is
available from the British Library.

ISBN 978-1-84533-371-3

While all reasonable care has been taken
during the preparation of this edition,
neither the publisher, editors, nor the
authors can accept responsibility for any
consequences arising from the use thereof
or from the information contained therein.

Commissioning Editor: Becca Spry
Art Director: Tim Foster
Deputy Art Director: Yasia Williams-
  Leedham
Designer: Miranda Harvey
Photography: Chris Terry
Project Editor: Ruth Patrick
Editor: Susan Fleming
Home Economist: Sara Lewis
Production Manager: Peter Hunt
Index: Helen Snaith

Typeset in Candida

Colour reproduction by Sang Choy,
Singapore
Printed and bound by Toppan, China

contents

introduction

Food has always been a pleasure and I definitely eat for enjoyment before necessity. My style of cooking is about the whole package: a good bottle of wine, good company, a grappa or two. Most importantly, I want honest food cooked to be enjoyed rather than to impress; no silly garnishes or clever ways to mess around with the ingredients. There are two camps a chef can belong to. There are those hell-bent on stars and other accolades, who obsessively chase perfection and applause. Then there are those chefs who take a more relaxed approach to cooking and focus on the provenance of the food.

I was first inspired to become a chef because of the excitement and unpredictability that Marco Pierre White brought to the profession, and my first proper job was working for him at The Oak Room. Then it was the influence and creative talents of stellar chefs Alastair Little, Simon Hopkinson and another food hero whose kitchens I worked in, Sally Clarke, that gave me the additional skills and knowledge to set up on my own.

Even so, a wave of panic washed over me as I took the tube into Soho for my last shift at Alastair Little's. From now on I wouldn't be grabbing a double espresso every day on my way down Frith Street and the late edition *Evening Standard* on my way home. I was swapping the buzz of Soho for the bleating of sheep to set up my own place in a very small village near to where I grew up in Monmouthshire.

It took a long time to adjust to the change in pace and the pressures of my own business. But we eventually started reaping the rewards of our efforts, with the help of an Italian coffee machine (which cost more than my car), some pure Arabica coffee and a loyal band of family and regular customers, who encouraged me to concentrate on the food I wanted to cook and not be pressured into producing a menu that tried to please everyone.

As it turned out, a lot of the best suppliers I'd been using in London were based in or around Monmouthshire. At The Foxhunter, it's not hard to keep the food miles down when there are farms all around producing some of the best meat and dairy products in the world. In Britain, 'local' and 'seasonal' have become buzz-words in the restaurant business, in danger of losing their meaning. But in most of Europe – and luckily in some parts of this country – they still just mean producing and selling food the way it has been for centuries.

Being based here, eating locally and seasonally comes naturally. Why buy lamb from New Zealand when some of the best lamb to be found is in our village, or even asparagus from Evesham when the stuff grown in Nantyderry is just as good? But I don't buy local just to reduce air and road miles, for me it's also about building up a good relationship with local farmers and suppliers and supporting the local community as a whole.

I know everyone keeps banging on about it, but it really is so important to eat within the seasons. For hundreds of years, buying the ingredients when supply was plentiful and at the peak of quality was the most economical way of sourcing food. But these days

it also helps promote a better understanding of the environment and gives farmers an incentive to focus on quality, not quantity. Most excitingly though, as a chef, it requires me to be more creative with each season and to come up with appetizing menus at all times of the year, which can be tricky in January.

In the same vein, a real incentive for me is encouraging the reintroduction of old varieties of fruit and veg, which can be quite exciting, I'll have you know! The different flavours, textures and aromas that the more unusual varieties can bring to a dish are well worth the effort of sourcing them in the first place. There are quite a few local suppliers who use bio-dynamic methods. This can sound like hocus-pocus, but it does seem to produce the most wonderful looking and tasting results.

We also favour rare animal breeds that have genuinely faced extinction in the weirdly insane mission to keep bringing food costs down. Longhorn beef and Middle White pork are regulars on my menu; I have yet to find better for flavour. A lot of my recipes are simple to make and so the hard bit is making sure the quality of the ingredients is up to scratch, and I find sourcing locally and in season are the best ways to achieve it.

For a break from the kitchen, I take the children down to the Severn to pick the marsh samphire and sea-beet, which go so very well with our sweet, local lamb, or up on to the Blorenge to pick the whimberries, which spice up a simple crumble and make a really subtle sorbet. Our foraging trips, followed by a wild food lunch at The Foxhunter – where your finds are served up with other wild food dishes on the menu – are popular as much for the glorious local surroundings as my food.

I am really pleased with the following we have built up at the restaurant, and people seem to appreciate the balance between simple rustic dishes and some of my more unusual offerings. I haven't exchanged the espressos for a nice cup of tea yet, but after a day fishing on the River Usk or a particularly fruitful foraging trip, I don't really miss the fumes and bustle of Frith Street any more.

Matt Tebbutt

overleaf *Lunch with my wife Lisa, and three of the most inspiring food heroes, Alastair Little, Simon Hopkinson and Tom Parker Bowles. All of them share my enthusiasm for long lunches, great food and lots of really good wine!*

JANUARY • FEBRUARY

JANUARY AND FEBRUARY

The beginning of the year seems to call for a lighter approach to cooking. A cleansing of the system is required after the full-on festive period. But cold, crisp days still demand an element of traditional comfort food, like Welsh cawls and French brandades, sticky braises and nursery puddings, but maybe with less of the rich excess of the past month or two.

Lighter dishes tend to come naturally at this time of year, as there's less choice of locally sourced food and wild ingredients, but don't worry, there's still lots to get excited about. There's an abundance of healthy cold-water fish and the big exception to the 'eating in season' rule – forced rhubarb, so succulent and versatile to use.

I don't cut down the calories too drastically though, and chocolate features quite prominently on my pudding menu – and I think justifiably so – during these cold months. You have to keep the pleasure in cooking and it's easy to become bored with slightly tired pears and apples that seemed much more appealing in the previous autumn.

I also like to make the most of the Seville and blood oranges that have so many great uses. As well as marmalades, sorbets and tarts, I knock up a bitter orange liqueur just after Christmas, which stews away in the cellar until June, when it goes on my menu as a wonderful summer apéritif.

ham hock, mustard fruits and fresh herb sauce

Ham hock is relatively inexpensive and like other similar cuts should be slow-cooked, but the time invested is well worth the trouble. This is incredibly simple, but delivers the most delicious results and utilizes the cooking liquor that is so often discarded. You could make the mustard fruits yourself but it is time-consuming and there are some exceptionally good bottled varieties around.

serves 4–6

2 salted ham hocks
4 celery sticks, cut in half
3 carrots, cut down the middle
lengthways
2 large white onions, peeled
and halved
1 twig bay leaves
3–4 cloves
1 tsp black peppercorns
1 garlic bulb, cut in half
1 handful of parsley stalks
3–4 sprigs of fresh thyme

Fresh herb sauce
1 tbsp red wine vinegar
1 tbsp Dijon mustard
extra virgin olive oil
½ bunch each of fresh tarragon, mint,
basil and flat-leaf parsley, chopped
1 tbsp capers
1 red onion, peeled and diced
salt and pepper

1 x 400g jar mustard fruits (mostarda di
cremona, bottled is fine), to serve

Put the ham hocks in cold water in a saucepan and bring to the boil. Boil for 1 minute, remove and change the water. Cover again in cold water and repeat the process twice more. This will rid the ham of any excess salt.

Throw the veg in the pan along with all the other aromatics and bring to the boil. Simmer for 1½–2 hours or more or until the small bone at the top of the hock can be pulled free. Remove from the heat and allow the ham to cool in the stock.

When cool enough to handle, pick over the meat and remove excess fat and sinew. Keep the meat in nice big chunks, do not shred. Set aside.

Ladle out about 2–3 ladles of the cooking liquor, about 500ml, and pour through a fine-meshed sieve. Reduce in a pan by half to concentrate the flavours. Cool this stock in the fridge until required.

To make the herb sauce, mix the red wine vinegar, Dijon mustard and about 6 tbsp extra virgin olive oil in a bowl. Stir in the herbs, capers and the onion. Season and add more olive oil to bind. Allow to mingle at room temperature for a while to improve the flavours.

When ready to serve, simply heat the reduced stock and put the ham in it. Simmer for a few minutes and serve with some mustard fruits and a spoon of the herb sauce.

cawl cennin, salt bacon and caerphilly cheese

This is a traditional Welsh dish, the equivalent I suppose of the Irish stew. Everyone has an opinion on what should and shouldn't go in the pot, as this used to be a way to use up leftovers and odd cuts of meat, but whatever you use, it will hit the spot.

serves 4

5–6 leeks, cleaned and finely sliced
salt and pepper
400g Caerphilly cheese
fresh crusty bread, to serve

Stock
1 x 2kg piece of salted bacon
1 small bunch of fresh thyme
3–4 bay leaves
1 tsp black peppercorns
1 garlic bulb, cut in half
2 onions, peeled and cut in half
2 carrots, cut in rough chunks
4–5 celery sticks, cut in rough chunks

Firstly, make the stock by putting the salted bacon in a saucepan with all the other stock ingredients. Cover with cold water and bring to the boil. Turn down the heat to a gentle simmer, cover and cook for a further 2–3 hours, skimming frequently.

Remove from the heat and allow to settle. Pass the liquid through a very fine sieve and chill overnight. Reserve the cooked bacon.

The next day, remove the fat from the stock, taste and reduce if necessary to the required taste. Be careful not to make the stock too salty.

Strain into a clean pan and throw in the sliced leeks. Simmer until tender, for about 4–5 minutes. At this point, add some chunks of the cooked bacon to the soup. This is optional, as all the flavour is now in the stock.

Season, only if necessary. Spoon into individual bowls and crumble the cheese over the top. Serve with fresh crusty bread.

cauliflower soup with black pudding and dill

The black pudding and dill add some colour and texture to this seasonal soup.

serves 4–6

2 small cauliflowers
1 white onion, peeled and chopped
90g butter
1 sprig of fresh thyme
2 garlic cloves, peeled and crushed
1 bunch of fresh dill, fronds and stalks separated
1 bay leaf
milk, to cover
200g black pudding
2 shallots, peeled and finely chopped
salt and pepper

Cut out the stalks of the cauliflowers and grate the rest into a bowl.

In a saucepan, sweat off the chopped onion in a third of the butter with the thyme, garlic and dill stalks. Add the grated cauliflower and bay leaf, and sweat off for a further 5 minutes. Cover with milk and simmer for 25 minutes.

Meanwhile, take the black pudding flesh out of the skins, break it down and mix with about 1 tbsp of the chopped dill fronds and all the chopped shallot. Form into balls the size of an old penny. Pan-fry these balls until cooked through in half the remaining butter and keep warm.

Season the cauliflower mixture to taste. Purée with the remaining cold butter and pass through a fine sieve. Heat through, then portion into individual bowls. Place the black pudding balls in the soup and garnish with dill sprigs.

quails roasted in vine leaves with brandy

This is a recipe from our forager Raoul's family cookbook, one of many great dishes he has shared with us over the years.

serves 4

8 quails, rinsed
salt and pepper
8 vine leaves (1 x 225g vacuum pack)
olive oil
50ml brandy
450ml chicken stock (*see* page 296)
4 slices of fried bread, halved

Preheat the oven to 180°C/350°F/gas mark 4.

Season each quail, wrap in a vine leaf, drizzle with a little olive oil and put in a roasting tin. Roast in the preheated oven for about 10 minutes.

Deglaze the tin with the brandy and flame to remove the alcohol. Add the chicken stock to the quails. Open out the vine leaves so the breasts can brown and roast in the oven for a further 10 minutes. Remove from the oven and allow to rest a little, catching any juices in the pan.

Top each piece of fried bread with a roasted quail. Serve with the meat juices.

marinated quail salad

Try and find time to marinate the quail. It takes a bit of forward planning but ultimately it is a very simple and extremely satisfying dish.

serves 4

4 quails, spatchcocked (ask your butcher to do this) and rinsed
1 tsp salt
2 tsp brown sugar
2 fresh red chillies, chopped
50g fresh coriander stalks and roots, finely chopped
100ml rice wine vinegar
vegetable oil
50g picked fresh coriander leaves
25g picked fresh mint leaves
4 pinches of sesame seeds
200g Japanese mooli or daikon radish, shredded
3–4 tbsp soy sauce
juice of 1 lime

Put the quails in a suitable dish. Mix the salt, sugar, chillies, coriander stalks and roots together, cover and marinate the quail in this for 3 to 4 days in the fridge.

Preheat the oven to 180°C/350°F/gas mark 4.

When ready to cook, pan-fry the quail to seal in a little oil, then put into the preheated oven for 5–6 minutes. Remove and allow to rest.

Make a salad from the coriander and mint leaves, sesame seeds and shredded radish. Dress with the soy sauce, lime juice and quail juices from the pan.

Portion the quail. Cut in half lengthways, remove the legs, and serve 2 legs and 2 breasts per person. Arrange on a plate with the dressed salad.

duck legs in brine

This is a great way of preserving meats, pork for rillettes, beef brisket for salt beef or, in this example, duck legs. Simply drop the meat into the brine, put in the fridge and forget about it for a couple of weeks. The brine adds a flavour to the meat that no marinade or fancy sauce could ever bring.

serves 4

4 duck legs, rinsed
stock vegetables (2 celery sticks, 1 large white onion, 1 large carrot, 1 leek)
an assortment of hard herbs such as thyme or rosemary, no more than a
   100g bunch, say

Brine
1.7 litres water
280g rock salt
280g brown sugar, or muscovado for a more caramelly taste
25g saltpetre (optional, available from chemists)
plus any herbs and spices you fancy (2–3 bay leaves, 1 sprig of rosemary,
   1 small bunch of thyme, 1 tsp black peppercorns, 1 piece of mace, a few
   juniper berries)

Put the brine ingredients into a saucepan, bring to the boil and simmer for 20 minutes to infuse. Skim and cool.

Then add the duck legs (or any other meat you would like to try) to the brine. Submerge the meat totally under some baking paper and a couple of heavy plates. Leave for anything between 2 and 6 weeks in the fridge.

When the duck is suitably brined, remove and plunge into water. Leave for 24 hours, changing the water every 6–8 hours.

When ready to cook, put the duck legs into a saucepan of cold water and bring gently to the boil. Remove the legs and pour the water away. This 'purging' will rid the legs of any excess salt. Now put the meat back into cold water, this time with the stock vegetables and the hardy herbs, and bring to the boil once again. Turn down the heat and simmer, uncovered, for 1½–2 hours until the duck legs are tender but not falling off the bone. Leave to cool in the stock. This all sounds like hard work but it really is worth the end result.

What you will finally be left with is a duck leg that resembles ham in appearance, which has a delicately herby, lightly seasoned taste, not unlike a gammon or bacon. The legs can be eaten cold or reheated in a little bit of the cooling stock.

guineafowl confit

It's the same process for duck legs, chicken legs, pork belly or even lamb breast...

serves 4

guineafowl legs, rinsed
2 handfuls of rock salt
1 tbsp black peppercorns, crushed
1 star anise
1 garlic bulb, smashed up
a few bay leaves
a few sprigs of fresh thyme
enough duck fat to cover, up to 1 litre, depending on size of pan

Lay the guineafowl legs in a tray. Throw over the salt. Lightly crush or break up the aromatics and scatter over. Leave for 24 hours covered in the fridge.

The next day take the legs out of the salt and rinse very quickly under running water. Pat dry.

Put the herbs used in the salting into a saucepan, add the guineafowl legs and cover with the fat. Bring to a gentle boil, cover and simmer for 1–1½ hours until tender. Leave to cool in the fat. This confit can now be stored in the fridge for many weeks, sealed by the fat.

To reheat simply remove the legs, put into a cold pan, skin-side down and place in a hot oven at 200°C/400°F/gas mark 6 for 20 minutes or so until crisp and brown.

soup paysanne with guineafowl confit

You can substitute other confits. It doesn't have to be guineafowl, of course, but I think this makes an interesting change from duck.

serves 4 as a main course, up to 8 as a starter

2 tbsp duck fat

1 white onion, peeled and finely chopped

2 carrots, diced

4 celery sticks, diced (keep the leaves for garnish)

1 garlic bulb, cut in half widthways

30g fresh thyme

a few bay leaves

salt and pepper

150g bacon lardons

2 large handfuls of button mushrooms, quartered

1 Savoy cabbage (use only the outer darker leaves, the first few layers of the cabbage), finely shredded

250g cooked Puy or Umbrian lentils

1 litre guineafowl or chicken stock (*see* page 296)

4 confit guineafowl legs (*see* page 26)

Heat the duck fat in a large saucepan and throw in the white onion, carrot and celery. Cook without colour for 15–20 minutes. Add the garlic, thyme and bay leaves. Season carefully at this point. Throw in the bacon and cook for a further 5 minutes. Stir in the button mushrooms and Savoy cabbage. Stir from time to time for another 10 minutes.

Now add the lentils and the stock, bring to a simmer, taste and season. Finally, flake the guineafowl meat into the soup base. Warm through gently for a few minutes and serve. Garnish with some chopped celery leaves.

pickled mullet with pine nuts and raisins

This is based on a traditional Italian recipe using sardines. It is both practical, in terms of preserving the fish, and delicious in its own right. Never serve straight from the fridge.

serves 4

2 large red mullet, filleted into 4 pieces and rinsed
350ml olive oil
1 sprig of fresh rosemary
2 large white onions, peeled and cut into semi-circles about 5mm thick
1 handful of raisins
a few bay leaves
150ml white wine
1 slug of white wine vinegar
1 tsp each of salt and caster sugar
3 tbsp pine nuts, toasted
1 handful of flat-leaf parsley, roughly chopped

In a lightly oiled hot frying pan, seal off the fish for 1 minute per side, remove and place on a tray to cool.

Pour the olive oil into a saucepan and warm with the rosemary sprig. Throw in the onions and soften, which will take about 10 minutes.

Add the raisins, bay leaves, white wine and white wine vinegar. Season with the salt and sugar and stew for about 5 minutes. Taste and adjust the sweetness or acidity until nicely balanced, then sprinkle in the pine nuts.

While still warm, pour the onion-vinegar mix over the fish. This will continue to cook the fish due to the acidity and the residual heat.

The fish is best served the same day at room temperature, with a scattering of parsley. It will keep for a few days in the fridge but always serve at room temperature, never cold. The dish needs no other accompaniment.

mussel and saffron brandade, with bacon crumbs

Rich, fat mussels, soft melting potato and the crunch of smoked bacon – just a great combination of textures and flavours.

serves 4

1kg mussels (shelled weight, 2kg in shell), scrubbed and debearded
350ml white wine
1 bay leaf
2 sprigs of fresh thyme
200ml double cream
100ml olive oil
½ garlic bulb, cut in half again
1 pinch of good saffron strands
700g mash (*see* page 297)
salt and pepper
4 medium free-range eggs, soft-poached

Bacon crumbs
2 rashers of streaky bacon
olive oil
Japanese breadcrumbs (available at good delis and oriental supermarkets), or normal breadcrumbs

Begin by tapping each mussel with a knife, discarding any that do not close. Steam the mussels in a pan in the white wine with the bay leaf and thyme for 3–4 minutes, covered, until the mussels open. Discard any that do not open fully. Strain and reserve the juices. Remove the mussel meat from the shells when cool. Set aside. Strain the mussel liquor through a sieve or kitchen cloth to remove any grit.

Warm the cream, olive oil and garlic in a saucepan to infuse, with the saffron. Stir the infused cream bit by bit into the warm mashed potato, plus some of the mussel liquor, until you have a soft but not too wet mixture. The consistency should hold its own weight. Taste and season, making sure you have included all the saffron filaments. Stir in the mussel meat. Keep warm.

To make the bacon crumbs, fry off the bacon in a little oil in a frying pan until crisp. Remove from the pan, then throw in the breadcrumbs, toss and toast until golden. Blitz the bacon in a food processor with the crumbs. Reserve while you poach the eggs.

Serve the mussel brandade with a soft-poached egg, and some toasted bacon crumbs.

eggs poached in red wine

The red wine colours the eggs so the dish looks quite dramatic. This makes a great cold-weather supper dish.

serves 4

150g bacon, cut into lardons
150g button mushrooms, cut in half
1 onion, peeled and chopped
50g unsalted butter
1 bottle deep, rich red wine
250ml beef consommé or stock (*see* page 294)
2 large handfuls of fresh large-leaf spinach, or 4 bags baby leaf spinach
salt and pepper
4 large free-range eggs
1 splash of red wine vinegar
1 bay leaf
4 slices of fried bread, to serve

In a frying pan, fry the lardons, mushrooms and onion in the butter until all are golden. Pour in a glass of the red wine and reduce until virtually nothing. Add the stock and reduce by half. Reserve until later, keeping it warm.

Wash the spinach well, then put in a hot, dry saucepan with only the water clinging to its leaves. Season and heat until just wilted. Put to one side and keep warm.

Now poach the eggs. Bring the rest of the red wine to the simmer in a small saucepan, and add the red wine vinegar and bay leaf. Gently swirl the wine mix and carefully drop the eggs in for about 4 minutes. The eggs must be submerged. Remove and drain each egg on kitchen paper and season the top.

To assemble, put a small amount of spinach on each plate, top with an egg and spoon over the bacon garnish and sauce. Serve with warm fried bread.

prawns with romesco sauce

This sauce makes quite a lot; but it gets better with age, and will keep in the fridge quite happily for a week or more. I mainly use it with prawns or squid, occasionally langoustines, but you can experiment.

serves 4

600g prawns, rinsed
olive oil, for shallow-frying
100ml sherry
4 tbsp chopped fresh parsley

Romesco sauce (makes more than you need here)
2 fresh red chilli peppers
2 red capsicum peppers
4 garlic cloves
100ml extra virgin olive oil
1 tsp caster sugar
1 tbsp sherry vinegar
100g blanched whole almonds, toasted
salt

Preheat the oven to 180°C/350°F/gas mark 4.

For the sauce, roast the peppers, chilli and garlic, in a little olive oil in a roasting tin in the preheated oven until the peppers start to caramelize, about 15–20 minutes. When cool enough to handle, deseed the chillies and peppers, peel the garlic and chop everything.

Put in a food processor, add the extra virgin oil, sugar and vinegar, and blitz to a paste. Add the almonds and season with salt. Again blitz to a coarse paste.

In a frying pan, sauté the prawns off in a little olive oil. Add the sherry and reduce for a minute. Add 4 tbsp of the romesco sauce, along with the parsley. Mix and heat through briefly, then serve.

curried lamb sweetbreads

I like to use offal on my menus, and I'm always pleasantly surprised how many people order sweetbreads.

serves 4

800g lamb's sweetbreads, trimmed of fat and gristle, and rinsed
50g butter
1 tsp mild curry powder
100g plain flour, for dusting

Curry cream sauce
25g butter
1 white onion, peeled and chopped
salt and pepper
1 garlic clove, peeled and minced
½ tbsp Madras curry powder
125ml vermouth
1 bay leaf
250ml double cream
90g raisins, soaked in warm water

Sprout leaves
1 small knob of butter
4 large handfuls of Brussels sprouts, separated into leaves, washed
about 40g split blanched almonds, toasted

First make the sauce. Melt the butter in a saucepan, throw in the onion and sweat for 10 minutes. Add a pinch of salt, the garlic and curry powder and cook out for 2 minutes. Now add the vermouth and bay leaf, and boil to reduce by half. Add the cream and bring to the boil. Strain if desired and reserve. Taste for seasoning. At this point add the raisins. Keep warm.

For the sweetbreads, melt the butter in a frying pan until foaming. Dust the sweetbreads with the curry powder and flour and gently sauté until golden brown all over. This should take up to 5–6 minutes. Keep warm on the side of the stove.

Finally in a frying pan add a small knob of butter and sauté the sprout leaves, just to wilt but still retain their texture and shape. This will take 2–3 minutes. Season.

To serve, pile the sprout leaves in the middle of the plate with the sweetbreads. Spoon the sauce over the top and around. Sprinkle with the toasted almonds.

pork belly, marrowfat peas and cornichon vinaigrette

I know many people find the thought of eating fatty meat unappealing, but the flavours you get from a good-quality pork belly are worth being brave for, I promise.

serves 4 as a main course

1 whole pork belly (approx. 2kg)
salt and pepper
1 lemon, cut in half
cornichon vinaigrette (see page 35)

Marinade
2 dried bay leaves
1 bunch of fresh oregano
1 garlic bulb, smashed up
200ml olive oil

Marrowfat peas
1 x 500g bag dried peas
1 celery stick
1 carrot
1 onion
1 garlic bulb, cut in half
1 bay leaf
a few sprigs of fresh thyme or another hard herb

In a pestle and mortar, pound the marinating ingredients together with the olive oil to make a paste. Rub the paste into the belly pork, cover and leave in the fridge for a few hours or overnight (do not season with salt at this point).

Preferably soak the peas overnight in cold water. If you're unable to do so, bring them up to the boil in a saucepan of cold water. Remove the pan from the heat, cover and leave for 1 hour in the hot liquid, then drain and now treat the peas as if they were soaked.

Set the oven high, to about 220°C/425°F/gas mark 7. Season the pork with salt and roast on a rack over a water bath for 30 minutes or so to start the crackling off. (The water bath stops the oven filling with smoke from dripping fat.)

Turn the oven down to 160°C/325°F/gas mark 3, and roast the pork slowly for an hour. Squeeze the lemon over the skin and continue to roast for a further hour (the lemon acid will help to crisp the skin).

While the pork is roasting, put the soaked peas in a saucepan, throw in the vegetables and herbs, and simmer for 1–1 ½ hours until the peas are soft. Remove the stock veg and squeeze the garlic into the peas. The peas should be of a good dolloping consistency: if too thick, add a little more water and adjust the seasoning.

Remove the pork from the oven and allow to rest for 30 minutes. The meat should be meltingly tender. If the skin is still not crisp enough, try blistering under a hot grill or cook the pork for a further 20 minutes at full whack. Please note that some pork, especially supermarket pork, is full of water and the skin is very hard to crisp up.

Serve the pork sliced with the peas and cornichon vinaigrette.

cornichon vinaigrette

This is very good with the pork belly and marrowfat peas on page 34. It makes more than you need for one serving, but it keeps extremely well in the fridge if left undisturbed under the oil.

serves at least 4
1 handful of baby cornichons
1 tbsp baby capers
300ml peanut oil
100ml sherry vinegar
1 tsp Dijon mustard
salt and pepper

Simply dice the cornichons and mix in a bowl with the capers. Mix together with the peanut oil, sherry vinegar, Dijon mustard and salt and pepper to taste. Leave for a while at room temperature to allow the flavours to mingle.

overleaf *James Swift, of Trealy Farm in Monmouth, with his rare-breed pigs, that will eventually end up as some exceptional charcuterie.*

veal kidneys in bacon and cabbage broth with thyme dumplings

Thoroughly tasty and warming – this is healthy comfort food. Veal kidneys can be quite expensive for offal, but they are worth the money. If your budget doesn't stretch to veal, then lamb's kidneys can be used in the same way.

serves 4

2 large veal kidneys, rinsed and sliced through crossways (white fat and muscle tissue removed) into 1cm thickness
salt and pepper
fresh horseradish or mustard, to serve

Broth
2 white onions, peeled and diced
50g unsalted butter
150g good-quality farmhouse-style bacon, diced
1 garlic bulb, cut in half
a few sprigs of fresh thyme
2–3 bay leaves

350g potatoes, peeled, diced and washed of starch
1.25 litres chicken stock or light veal stock (*see* pages 296 and 294)
1 Savoy cabbage, shredded

Thyme dumplings
1 shallot, peeled and finely diced
30g butter
1 garlic clove, peeled and crushed
1 tbsp chopped fresh thyme leaves
100g shredded suet
100g self-raising flour
100g fresh breadcrumbs
2 medium eggs, beaten

To make the broth, firstly sweat the onion gently in the butter in a saucepan until soft but not coloured. Add the diced bacon and continue to cook. Throw in the garlic, thyme and bay leaves, then stir in the diced potatoes. Cook for 5 minutes or so, then add 1 litre of the stock and bring to the boil. Simmer for 30 minutes. Season to taste.

Meanwhile, make the dumplings. Sweat the shallot in the butter in a frying pan until soft, then stir in the garlic and thyme, and season. Mix this with the suet, flour and breadcrumbs. When cool enough, add the eggs. Mix together well. Roll into balls the size of pickled onions and poach very gently in the remaining hot chicken stock. The dumplings will take anywhere from 25–35 minutes, depending on the thickness. They should be slightly swollen and light to eat, not stodgy in any way. Reserve somewhere warm until the bacon and cabbage broth is ready.

After 30 minutes, stir the shredded cabbage into the broth and continue to simmer for a few minutes. Now drop in the kidneys and continue to cook for 4–5 minutes. At this point it is very important not to boil the stock or the kidneys will toughen.

Serve the broth with the thyme dumplings and offer some fresh horseradish or mustard on the side.

pot-roast pheasant with smoked bacon and cream

If you are wary of cooking pheasant, this it is a good way to retain moisture in the meat. The dish is very satisfying on a cold evening.

serves 2

50g butter
1 whole pheasant, rinsed
salt and pepper
1 white onion, peeled and cut into 1cm dice
2 celery sticks, cut into 1cm dice
1 garlic bulb, cut in half
50g smoked bacon, diced
200ml white wine
2 bay leaves
200ml double cream
a few sprigs of fresh thyme

Preheat the oven to 200°C/400°F/gas mark 6.

Heat the butter in a casserole. Season the bird, seal off in the butter on both sides and remove from the pan. Reserve.

Throw the onion, celery, garlic and smoked bacon into the casserole, and sweat off for about 10 minutes. Add the wine and stir in without reducing, then add the bay leaves, thyme and cream and bring up to the boil. Add the pheasant.

Place the casserole in the preheated oven and cook for 15 minutes or until cooked. Remove and leave to rest for 10 minutes.

Joint the pheasant and warm through in the sauce. Serve with pumpkin and ginger purée (*see* page 199).

rock salmon, marinated beetroot and black pepper

Rock salmon or dogfish is quite hard to find these days as it is rarely landed because of its little or no commercial value. This is a shameful waste as rock salmon has a taste and texture not unlike eel and can carry strong flavours. Your fishmonger should be able to source some for you given a little notice.

serves 4

4 x 200g rock salmon fillets, rinsed
salt and pepper
olive oil
4 tbsp crème fraîche, to serve

Marinated beetroot
4 beetroot, cooked and peeled
1 tsp coriander seeds, lightly toasted and crushed
1 handful of fresh coriander leaves, roughly chopped
1 garlic clove, peeled and finely chopped
1 splash of red wine vinegar
100ml extra virgin olive oil

Spiced oil
200ml olive oil
1 tsp black peppercorns, lightly crushed
½ tsp white peppercorns, lightly crushed
1 bay leaf
a few sprigs of fresh thyme
1 star anise

Firstly cut the beetroot into eighths and mix with the marinade ingredients. Leave at room temperature to marinate for a few hours.

To make the spiced oil, warm the ingredients together in a saucepan gently. Do not boil. Leave aside somewhere warm to infuse.

To cook the rock salmon, season and lightly oil the fish fillets, and grill or char-grill on both sides for a few minutes. (The fish is quite thin and will take no longer than 5 minutes from start to finish.)

To assemble the dish, scatter the beetroot on a plate with some of the marinade. Cut the fish fillets into smaller chunks and dot them around. Spoon over the spiced oil, being careful not to spoon out the bits. Finally add a dollop of crème fraîche.

roast pollack, spiced shrimp butter and seakale

Pollack is the sustainable alternative to the much-loved cod. It is currently more sustainable and equal in both size and stature to its now over-fished cousin. I've put seakale in here because it's a luxury ingredient that you rarely find in the shops, but is well worth seeking out. It is found for just a few weeks from the middle of February. If you can't find it, the shrimp butter will liven up any green accompaniment.

serves 4

4 x 230g pollack fillets, rinsed
salt
800g seakale
olive oil

Spiced shrimp butter
100g pre-cooked brown shrimps, peeled and rinsed
150g salted butter
1 tsp ground turmeric
1 tsp curry powder
1 tsp coriander seeds, crushed
2 tsp (20g approx.) grated fresh root ginger
1 tbsp chopped fresh coriander leaves
1 garlic clove, peeled and crushed
juice of ½ lemon

Mix all the spiced shrimp butter ingredients together, roll into a log and chill. The butter will keep for 3–4 days in the fridge.

Place the pollack fillets in a dish and lightly salt. Cover and leave for 30 minutes or so, until you are ready to cook. Trim and wash the seakale. In the short term, it is best kept in iced water. Preheat the oven to 180°C/350°F/gas mark 4.

Heat a non-stick and ovenproof frying pan to a high heat, and add a drop of olive oil to the pan. Pat the fish dry with some kitchen paper. Don't re-season, there is enough salt in the fish already. Lay the fish flesh-side down in the pan. Jostle about gently to prevent sticking and allow to colour on this side for 3–4 minutes until nicely golden. Now turn the fish over, put into the preheated oven and roast for a further 5–6 minutes until cooked through.

Meanwhile, drop the seakale into a saucepan of boiling salted water for a couple of minutes. Remove and drain.

Simply place the seakale alongside the fish, then slice a small amount of the butter over the fish. Allow to melt, then serve.

steamed sea bream, artichoke purée, kale, sage and capers

Steaming really accentuates all the subtle flavours of a beautiful piece of fresh fish. It's so simple as a main ingredient that you can add some great seasonal accompaniments to create the finished dish. The intensely rich artichoke purée perfectly complements the earthy flavour and texture of the kale.

serves 4

4 royal sea bream fillets, rinsed (black bream is also an option; farmed fish are OK but tend to be a little flabby)
salt and pepper
4 sage leaves
250g kale, washed and torn into smaller pieces
25g butter
1 squeeze of lemon juice
Jerusalem artichoke purée (*see* page 44)

Sage butter
100g unsalted butter
8 sage leaves
4 tsp small capers
a squeeze of lemon juice

To steam the fish, wrap each fillet in clingfilm with some light seasoning and a sage leaf, to make a parcel. Have your steamer boiling away and quickly add the fish fillets in one even layer (do not stack). Steam for about 7–10 minutes until the fish feels firm to the touch and has no 'give' to it. Remove and keep in the clingfilm somewhere warm until needed.

For the sage butter, put the butter and the sage leaves in a cold saucepan. Melt the butter until foaming gently and watch it very carefully. The butter will turn a lovely chestnut colour. Keep swirling the pan to move the milk solids about so they don't stick and burn. Working quickly, throw in the capers and a small squeeze of lemon and a pinch of salt, then remove from the heat.

In another saucepan, sauté the kale in the 25g butter for about 10 minutes, or until the kale has just wilted but still retains its texture, then season and add a few drops of lemon juice.

To assemble the dish, spoon the warmed purée on each plate then top with a little of the kale. Unwrap the fish and lay on top. Spoon over the caper and sage butter. Serve immediately.

jerusalem artichoke purée

One of the colder months' great treats, Jerusalem artichokes are a bit odd to look at and a bit fiddly to prepare, but if you can get over that, then they do deliver the most velvety-smooth, intensely flavoured soups and purées. It's delicious with the sea bream on page 42, but is also good with some scallops and caramelized garlic.

serves 6–8 (but will keep in the fridge for a day or two before discolouring)

750g Jerusalem artichokes

lemon juice or white wine vinegar

1 white onion, peeled and chopped

3 garlic cloves, peeled and roughly chopped

50g unsalted butter

2 sprigs of fresh thyme

1 bay leaf

100ml double cream

Firstly prepare the artichokes by peeling quickly and placing in some water with a lemon squeezed into it or a splash of white wine vinegar. The acid prevents the artichoke from turning black.

In a hot saucepan sweat the onion and garlic in the butter until translucent, without colour, for 10 minutes or so. Add the thyme and bay leaf. With a box grater or Japanese mandolin, quickly (but not jeopardizing your fingertips) slice or grate the raw artichokes into the onion and garlic. Stir in the artichokes to cover with the hot butter.

Add enough water to barely cover, then simmer for 10–20 minutes until the artichokes are cooked through. Add the cream, return to the boil, then purée in a food processor until smooth. Push through a sieve for an even smoother result.

spiced lentils with crème fraîche

This is a warming dish to accompany something like a simple roast chicken, but it is just as good eaten on its own from a big bowl with lots of fresh bread.

serves 4 as an accompaniment

50g unsalted butter
1 tsp each of ground coriander, turmeric
  and cumin
1 small knob of fresh root ginger, grated
2 garlic cloves, left whole
1 fresh red chilli, diced
½ white onion, peeled and finely diced
1 celery stick, finely diced
1 large chunk of smoked bacon (optional)
200g dried Puy or Umbrian lentils
salt and pepper
100g crème fraîche or soured cream, to serve

Melt the butter in a frying pan and when foaming, fry the ground spices to extract all their flavour. Toss in the ginger, garlic and chilli. Keep an eye on the pan to ensure the spices do not burn. Throw in the onion and celery, sweat down for 5 minutes and add the bacon, if desired. Then add the lentils and dry-fry them in the mix for a few minutes.

Cover with water and simmer for 15–20 minutes until just cooked. The lentils should retain their bite. Season and serve with a dollop of crème fraîche or soured cream.

savoyarde potatoes

Potato in a wicked form. It's very difficult to limit yourself to one, so always make spares...

serves 4

1 recipe Dauphinoise potatoes (*see* page 50)
200g Fontina, Gruyère or Emmental cheese, grated
8 slices of good-quality cured ham
700–800g bought or homemade puff pastry
1 medium egg plus 1 medium egg yolk, beaten together, for glazing

Start with your Dauphinoise potato at room temperature. Using a small circular cutter, cut out 8 potato rounds from the tray. I usually use an upturned individual pudding mould or a coffee cup. Top each round with grated cheese and wrap around a piece of ham.

Roll out the pastry to the thickness of a pound coin and cut out 8 discs with a small side-plate or saucer. Gently mould the pastry over the top of the potato and stretch to fit completely around each base. Pinch the pastry together and cut away any excess. Chill in the fridge for at least 30 minutes until ready to use.

Preheat the oven to 180°C/350°F/gas mark 4. Line a baking sheet with baking paper.

Place the wrapped potatoes on the baking sheet and glaze with the beaten egg. Cook for roughly 20 minutes until golden. Check the internal temperature by inserting a skewer into the middle of the potato to check it's hot.

With a sharp knife, cut each pastry casing down the middle to reveal the layers of potato, ham and cheese. This is good served with lamb or a simple chicken breast.

dauphinoise potatoes

Either serve immediately or chill and use to make Savoyarde potatoes...a delicious and quite naughty treat (see page 46). Don't worry about all the cream and butter, and don't try and reduce the quantities – that would spoil it. Just don't eat it every day!

serves 4–6

100g butter, plus extra for greasing
250ml milk
250ml double cream
1 garlic bulb, cut in half
a few sprigs of fresh thyme
3–4 bay leaves
salt and pepper
1 kg floury potatoes (eg Maris Piper or Golden Wonder), peeled

Preheat the oven to 200°C/400°F/gas mark 6, and butter a medium to large ovenproof dish (the potatoes should be no more than 5cm high in the dish).

Put the milk, cream, butter, garlic, thyme, bay leaves and some seasoning into a saucepan and bring to the boil. Simmer for 10 minutes to infuse the flavours.

Using a mandolin or very sharp knife, cut the potatoes into thin slices (so they bend when stood up).

Strain the milk mixture. Put back into the pan and add the sliced potatoes. Gently stir on the stove for 5–10 minutes to start cooking and release the starch (this will help weld the Dauphinoise together later). Tip into the buttered ovenproof dish with enough of the liquid to just cover. Too much liquid would result in a delicious-tasting but sloppy dish.

Cook uncovered in the preheated oven for 20–30 minutes, until the top starts to blister and colour. Turn the oven down to 150°C/300°F/gas mark 2, and continue to cook for another 40–50 minutes until a knife will easily and without resistance go through the potatoes. Remove and allow to rest a little.

eve's pudding

I'm sure you'll know this one already but if, like me, you haven't made it in years, here's a reminder.

serves 4

6 large Bramley apples
100g unsalted butter, plus extra for greasing
150g raisins
50g soft brown sugar
50g caster sugar
2 medium eggs
100g self-raising flour
Jersey cream of custard, to serve

Preheat the oven to 200°C/400°F/gas mark 6.

Peel, core and chop the apples and place them in a buttered medium ovenproof dish. Scatter the raisins over the top.

Cream the butter and sugars together in a bowl until pale and most of the sugar has dissolved. Beat in the eggs, then carefully fold in the flour.

Pour this batter over the apples and bake in the preheated oven for 45 minutes or so until golden. Serve warm with Jersey cream or custard.

seville orange marmalade tart

The bitter Seville oranges marry perfectly with the sweet almondy flavours. This is essentially a jumped-up Bakewell tart!

serves 4–6

2 tbsp quick Seville orange marmalade (*see* page 59)
1 x 30cm pastry tart shell, uncooked (*see* page 144)

Frangipane
250g unsalted butter
250g caster sugar
250g ground almonds
4 medium eggs
clotted cream, to serve

To make the frangipane, beat or cream the butter and sugar in a food processor until the sugar has dissolved and the butter is pale. Turn the food processor speed down and add the ground almonds. Beat until just incorporated, then add the eggs one at a time so the mix doesn't split. Chill until ready to use.

Preheat the oven to 150°C/300°F/gas mark 2.

To assemble the tart, spread the marmalade on the base of the tart shell. Cover with the frangipane and bake in the preheated oven for 40 minutes or until the frangipane is set (an inserted knife should come out clean).

Serve warm with a dollop of clotted cream.

rhubarb compote, blood orange cream and ginger ice cream

If you dislike the colour of the cooked fruit you could retain the pinkness by adding a drop or two of Grenadine, but this is not necessary and won't give you the real feeling of home-made comfort food.

serves 4

Ginger ice cream
250ml full-fat milk
300ml double cream
1 vanilla pod, split lengthways
200g stem ginger, grated, with about 2 tsp of its syrup (or more, to taste)
3 medium egg yolks
85g caster sugar

Rhubarb compote
200ml ginger wine
a few strips of orange zest
75g soft light brown sugar
250g young pink rhubarb, cut into 3cm batons

Blood orange cream
150ml double cream
1 recipe blood orange curd (*see* page 75)

For the ice cream, heat the milk, cream, vanilla, ginger and syrup together in a saucepan. Whisk the egg yolks and sugar together in a bowl. Pour the milk mix over the eggs and sugar and return to the pan to thicken over a gentle heat. Remove from the stove, cool, then churn in the usual way in an ice-cream machine. When almost done, remove and decant into a suitable container to the freezer.

For the compote, bring the ginger wine, zest and sugar to the boil in a saucepan. Turn the heat down, throw in the rhubarb and cook gently until tender, no longer than 3–5 minutes. This is compote, so don't be alarmed when the rhubarb starts to break down. Reserve the stewed fruit until later.

For the blood orange cream, whip the double cream to soft peaks and fold in enough of the curd to taste.

To assemble, sit a ball or dollop of ice cream in a bowl, spoon round the rhubarb and carefully spoon over some of the blood orange cream. You can serve with biscuits (*see* the recipes for amaretti or hazelnut shortbread on pages 291 and 187).

vin santo, pine nut
and olive oil cake

Everyone has a version of this classic olive oil cake recipe, and this one is essentially borrowed from Alastair Little's Keep it Simple *(who in turn borrowed it from Alice Waters), with a few small changes of my own. The success of the dish lies very much in the quality of the olive oil used.*

serves 8–10

4 medium eggs

125g caster sugar

finely grated zest of 1 lemon and 1 orange

125g plain flour

6 tbsp Vin Santo

3 tbsp best-quality extra virgin olive oil

50g pine nuts

icing sugar, for dusting

crème fraîche or fruit compote, to serve

Preheat the oven to 150°C/300°F/gas mark 2. Grease and flour a 28cm cake tin.

In a food processor, whisk the eggs and sugar for about 10 minutes until pale. Add both the zests.

Sift the flour on to a piece of baking paper. Turn the food processor down, quickly slide in the flour and pour in the sweet wine and olive oil. Turn off the machine and continue to gently fold the mix together.

Pour the mix into the prepared tin. Bake in the preheated oven for 25–35 minutes or until a knife inserted comes out clean. Remove the cake from the tin and allow to cool.

Scatter over the pine nuts, dust with icing sugar and glaze briefly with a blowtorch. Serve with a fruit compote or some Greek yogurt.

chocolate pudding and mascarpone ice cream

This is quite a light, delicate chocolate cake, with a deliciously molten interior.

makes 10–12 little puddings

Mascarpone ice cream
350ml water
150g caster sugar
finely grated zest and juice (about 75ml) of 2 lemons
400g mascarpone cheese

Chocolate pudding
250g dark chocolate, broken into pieces
250g unsalted butter
125g caster sugar
**1 tsp freshly ground star anise, sieved (remove seeds from the pod,
    and crush in a pestle and mortar)**
5 medium whole eggs
5 medium egg yolks
50g plain flour
1 pinch of salt

Start both ice cream and cake the day before. For the ice cream, simply boil the water, sugar and lemon zest in a saucepan. Once the sugar has dissolved, remove from the heat and stir in the mascarpone with the lemon juice. Cool and chill in an ice cream machine (be careful not to over-churn). Freeze in a suitable container.

For the chocolate pudding, melt the chocolate and butter in a bowl over a saucepan of hot water. Whisk up the sugar, powdered anise, eggs and egg yolks in a bowl until light and pale. Slowly add the melted chocolate to the egg-sugar mixture. Carefully fold in the flour and salt. Pour the mixture into little 200ml non-stick moulds, filling half of the way up. Chill in the fridge overnight.

Next day, preheat the oven to 180°C/350°F/gas mark 4.

Remove the pudding batter from the fridge, bring to room temperature and bake in the preheated oven for 10 minutes, no longer. The outside of the cake mix should be set firm yet the middle will remain molten.

Serve the cake hot with the mascarpone ice cream.

quick seville orange marmalade

This can be stored in the fridge and used in a multitude of ways. As well as the Seville orange marmalade tart on page 52, it can be put through custards for flavouring, chopped up and made into ice cream, interleaved through bread and butter pudding or layered through a chocolate tart. The syrupy bit of the marmalade is equally delicious spooned over something quite neutral like a pannacotta.

makes over 1 kg

6 Seville oranges
6 Seville oranges, juiced
900g caster sugar
900ml water
800ml Grand Marnier

Preheat the oven to 150°C/300°F/gas mark 2.

Slice the oranges through quite thinly, with the peel still on. Put them in a suitable ovenproof dish.

In a saucepan, bring the orange juice, sugar and water to the boil. Remove and add the booze. Pour over the oranges.

Lay a sheet of baking paper over the top and bake slowly in the preheated oven until the orange peel is soft, sweet and edible. This could take anything up to 1½–2 hours.

Leave to cool and refrigerate. Use as desired, hot or cold.

MARCH • APRIL

MARCH AND APRIL

By the beginning of March, most Brits have recovered from their excitement at the onset of roast parsnips and other root vegetables and are eager to move on to whatever spring has to offer. I've usually had my fill of kale by now, and there's still little else waiting in the wings on the greengrocery front.

So, evil of all evils, it's the season to import. It's either increased food miles or scurvy and kitchen boredom! These are the two dullest months on the chef's calendar. Inspiration runs low, pining for the first sights of spring, and menus tend to seek stimulation further afield to add a little zing to the palate. Don't get me wrong, I'm still buying all my meat, fish and dairy locally and it's not a case of selling out for two months of the year, you just need to supplement with a few more imported ingredients than are usually necessary.

When spring finally happens, the eagerness in the kitchen grows, the weather gets brighter and the mood lightens, and so does the countryside's natural larder. Wild foods begin to come into their own. Stinging nettles replace the peppery rocket we have been used to seeing for the last couple of months. Wild garlic and garlic flowers add freshness and colour to a whole array of dishes like risottos, soups and salads.

Then, before you know it, St George's Day is upon us and his namesake mushrooms and even the odd morel appear in the local woodland. All a sure sign that spring is here.

garlic soup with duck livers and garlic crisps

I do like soups with interesting 'bits' in (see the snails on page 66). If you're not with me on the combinations, then feel free to omit the offending elements or try substituting other flavours. The garlic soup is delicious on its own and not at all overpowering as might be expected.

serves 4

3 white onions, peeled and diced

2 bay leaves

2 sprigs of fresh thyme

50g unsalted butter

2 tbsp olive oil

1 garlic bulb, peeled and roughly chopped

2 large baking potatoes, peeled and diced

1 litre chicken or vegetable stock (*see* pages 296 and 297), or water

200ml double cream

salt and pepper

4 duck livers, rinsed

duck fat

red wine and crusty bread, to serve

Garlic crisps

4 garlic cloves, peeled and cut into slivers

1 sprig of fresh thyme

sea salt flakes

In a saucepan, sweat the onion, bay leaves and most of the thyme in 40g of the butter and the oil until the onion is soft but not coloured, about 10 minutes. Throw in the garlic, stir and cover, and cook gently for another 10 minutes, checking from time to time to prevent burning. Add the potato dice and stir together for 5 minutes.

Pour in the stock or water and bring to the boil. Cook for 20 minutes or until all the ingredients are soft. Add the cream and return to the boil. Remove from the heat and blend with the remaining butter. Push through a fine sieve. Season to taste.

For the crisps, gently heat up enough duck fat to cover the base of a small pan. Throw in the garlic slivers and thyme, and cook until golden brown. Remove with a slotted spoon and drain. Season with salt flakes. Reserve somewhere warm.

Finally season the duck livers with salt, pepper and the remaining fresh thyme. Fry them off in a little more duck fat until rare only, as the heat of the soup will continue their cooking, about 2 minutes. Slice the livers in half.

Pour the soup into warmed bowls, top each with 2 liver halves and sprinkle over the garlic crisps. Serve with a bottle of rich red wine and lots of warm crusty bread.

stinging nettle soup with toasted almonds and snails

An exciting spring soup, a little bit unusual but very much of the countryside. Wild nettles impart a particularly peppery taste, something that commercially grown rocket leaves rarely achieve. The combination of the almonds and snails really works for me, but I will forgive you if you omit the snails!

serves 4

2 white onions, peeled and diced
2 celery sticks, diced
2 leeks, cleaned and diced
1 garlic bulb, cut in half, with 1
  clove reserved for the snails
2 bay leaves
1 sprig of fresh thyme
50g unsalted butter
salt and pepper
3 large potatoes, peeled and diced
1 recipe chicken or vegetable stock
  (*see* pages 296 and 297)

150g young stinging nettles,
  tops only
1 large handful of freshly washed
  spinach
soured cream, to serve

Toasted almonds and snails

25g unsalted butter
80g blanched almonds, roughly chopped
16 large snails, cleaned and picked from
  the shells
1 tbsp finely chopped fresh parsley

In a saucepan, sweat the diced vegetables, garlic bulb halves, bay leaves and thyme in the butter until soft, about 15 minutes, then season with salt and pepper. Add the potato and stir frequently to prevent sticking. Cover with the stock and simmer for 30 minutes or until the potato is soft. Meanwhile blanch the nettles in boiling water and then refresh them in iced water. Squeeze the nettles dry. At this point you can touch them without stinging yourself; the dip in boiling water rids them of their prickly quality.

When the potato is soft, add the nettles along with the spinach. Stir briefly to wilt, then purée the soup in a food processor immediately. Chill over ice rapidly to preserve the colour. This does not affect the taste, it's for pure aesthetics. Push the soup through a sieve and keep to one side. Warm through when ready to serve.

For the snails, heat the butter in a small frying pan, then add the almonds and reserved garlic clove, finely chopped. Season and toss together, then immediately add the snails, throw in the parsley and stir until warmed through, about 2–3 minutes.

Put the hot soup into warm serving bowls and garnish with the sautéed snails and almonds. A little soured cream would not go amiss here.

Portuguese salt cod cakes

Working in London exposes you to many interesting characters. In one restaurant I worked in briefly, the pot-washer would bang on about his cooking skills being much better than those of us mere chefs. He gave us his recipe for salt cod cakes and, in all their simplicity, they may well prove that he was right.

serves 4–6

2 white onions, peeled and finely diced
3 garlic cloves, peeled and finely chopped
olive oil
600g salt cod, rinsed
500ml milk
1 bay leaf
2 sprigs of fresh thyme
400g freshly cooked mashed potato (*see* page 297)
3 medium egg yolks
1 handful of chopped fresh flat-leaf parsley
salt and pepper
plain flour
vegetable oil, for deep-frying
wedges of lemon and garlic mayonnaise (aïoli, *see* page 150), to serve

In a saucepan, sweat the diced onion and garlic in some olive oil for 10 minutes. Set aside.

Meanwhile, in another pan, poach the salt cod in the milk, with the bay leaf and thyme, until just cooked and able to be flaked, about 5–6 minutes. Remove the fish from the milk.

Stir the flaked fish into the mashed potato with the egg yolks and parsley. Fold in the onion and garlic, then check for seasoning. Shape into small 50p-sized balls and chill to firm up.

When ready to cook, heat the oil for deep-frying to 170°C/325°F (in a pot or wok), coat the cod cakes in a light dusting of flour and deep-fry until golden and hot in the middle. Check this by inserting a knife into the centre, it should come out very hot. If not, put the cod cakes back in the oil or through a hot oven for a few minutes.

Serve the cod cakes with nothing more than a wedge of lemon and some garlic mayonnaise, if desired.

soused herring with pickled cucumber and crème fraîche

Soused herring is a great standby as it keeps exceptionally well in the fridge and makes a perfect light lunch or supper dish. The important thing is to use herrings at their best.

serves 4

8 herring fillets, pin-boned and rinsed
4 tsp crème fraîche, to serve

Marinade
6 shallots, peeled and finely sliced into half-moons
salt and pepper
olive oil
1 tsp mixed peppercorns
1 star anise
a few parsley stalks
2 sprigs of fresh thyme

100ml white wine
50ml white wine vinegar
200ml salad oil (half veg/half olive), or neutral-tasting oil (like peanut)

Pickled cucumber
2 cucumbers
sea salt
400ml white wine vinegar
100g caster sugar, to taste
½ bunch of fresh dill, chervil or tarragon, chopped

Season the shallots with salt and sauté gently in a frying pan with a splash of olive oil for 5 minutes, just to take the edge off the onions. Add the aromatics, white wine, white wine vinegar and the salad oil. Bring to a gentle simmer and remove from the heat.

Lay the fillets of raw herring in a tray and pour over the marinade. The marinade must be hot – as the acidity of the marinade coupled with the gentle heat will cook the fish very delicately. Cover the baking tray and allow to cool naturally.

Meanwhile, make the pickled cucumber. Slice the cucumbers in half from head to toe, and remove the seeds with a spoon. Slice the cucumber by hand on a mandolin quite finely, about 2mm in width. Put into a colander and season heavily with sea salt. Leave for 1 hour to drain. After this time, squeeze the excess moisture from the cucumber with a tea-towel. Keep to one side.

Heat the white wine vinegar and sugar together in a saucepan until the sugar has dissolved. Taste and add more sugar if necessary. There should be a nice balance between acidity and sweetness. Pour over the cucumber, add the chopped herb of your choice and leave to marinate for half an hour or more.

Serve the pickled herrings along with the cucumber and some good-quality crème fraîche.

sautéed baby squid with bacon, red wine and coriander

Squid can stand up for itself, so big flavours don't worry it. This dish has a fabulous meaty quality to it, lifted gently by the fragrant coriander.

serves 4

300ml rich red wine
1 tbsp red wine vinegar
olive oil
salt and pepper
light brown sugar
8 whole rashers of pancetta or streaky bacon
1kg baby squid, cleaned (get your fishmonger to do this)
2–3 garlic cloves, peeled and cut into slivers
2 banana shallots, peeled and finely chopped
1 bunch of fresh coriander, finely chopped
15g unsalted butter
2 nice heads of red and white chicory, finely shredded lengthways, and
   a few nice sprigs of fresh coriander, to serve

For the red wine sauce, put the red wine in a small saucepan and reduce to about 3 tbsp. Remove from the heat and add to the red wine vinegar. Stir in 100ml of the olive oil to split the red wine. Add seasoning and sugar to taste. Set aside.

Heat about 1 tbsp of the olive oil in a non-stick frying pan and fry the bacon until crisp. Remove and keep warm to one side. Throw the squid into the bacon pan and sauté for a few minutes until cooked. Remove from the pan and keep warm, separate from the bacon.

Chuck the garlic, shallots and coriander into the pan, and stir round for a couple of minutes. Remove the pan from the heat and add a small knob of butter to create a sauce from the debris.

Arrange the red and white chicory shreds on serving plates, spoon over the squid and drizzle with the red wine sauce and the buttery pan juices. Garnish with the coriander sprigs and bacon.

cockle and wild sorrel risotto

Wild sorrel is fairly easy to find, and it works really well in fish dishes. Here I've combined it with fresh cockles to make a more unusual risotto.

serves 4

500g cockles, in shell, scrubbed and rinsed
125ml vermouth or white wine
1 white onion, peeled and finely diced
50g unsalted butter
50ml olive oil
200g arborio or carnaroli risotto rice
1 splash of Pernod (about 50ml)
400ml fish stock or chicken stock, hot (*see* pages 294 and 296)
1 large tbsp mascarpone cheese
1 large bunch (60–80g) of wild sorrel

Throw all the cockles and half of the vermouth into a large saucepan. Cover and cook until the shells open, about 5–6 minutes. Discard any that do not open. Pour the juice and all into a colander with a bowl underneath and allow to cool. Remove most of the cockle meat from the shells and set aside, but reserve some in shell to use as garnish.

Pour the juices through a sieve and a clean kitchen cloth into a jug to eliminate any grit. Reserve the in-shell cockles in a little of the cooking liquor.

In a shallow wide pan such as a wok, sweat the onion off in half the butter and all the olive oil for 5 minutes. Add the rice and stir about for a few minutes, then add the remaining vermouth. Reduce to almost nothing and add the Pernod – not too much – and reduce again.

Stir in a ladle of the hot stock and cook until all the liquid has gone. Add another ladle and continue the process for another 15 minutes or so until the rice is tender yet retaining a slight bite. Pour in the cockle liquor and reduce once more.

Stir in the mascarpone, remaining butter and the cockle meat. Warm through for a few minutes and finally stir in the chopped sorrel. Gently warm the still in-shell cockles in their liquor, and either scatter over or stir through. Serve immediately.

whisky potted shrimps

My mother used to make potted shrimps when I was a child. They're unashamedly rich and old-fashioned but really hit the spot! If you want to make it laborious, then you can peel your own shrimps, but if you don't, then the dish won't be any the poorer for it.

serves 4

1 large onion, peeled and diced
40g unsalted butter
200ml double cream
1½ tbsp whisky
about 280g shelled brown shrimps or small prawns, rinsed
2 tbsp finely chopped fresh parsley
about 100g Caerphilly cheese, grated

Preheat the grill to the highest temperature.

Sweat the diced onion in the butter in a frying pan until translucent, about 10 minutes. Add the double cream, bring to the boil and pour in the whisky. Boil off the alcohol for about a minute. Stir in the shrimps and parsley to bind with the cream mixture and remove from the heat.

Divide between small heatproof pots and sprinkle with the grated cheese.

Gratinate the tops under the grill until golden brown. Serve immediately.

picnic mushrooms

I can remember holidaying in France with my family and eating these straight from the polystyrene cups they sell in delicatessens. Every time I make them, I'm transported back to cloudy Brittany skies.

makes 1kg

600ml red wine vinegar
300ml red wine
1 tbsp sea salt
2 sprigs of fresh thyme
2 juniper berries, crushed
3 bay leaves
2–3 cloves
1kg small button mushrooms, cleaned
olive oil

Put the vinegar and wine in a non-reactive saucepan, and add all the aromatics. Heat to near boiling, then leave to infuse for 30 minutes.

Strain into a clean pan, add half the mushrooms and simmer for 10–15 minutes. Remove the mushrooms to a suitable container, using a slotted spoon. Put the remainder of the mushrooms in the spiced liquid and simmer for the same length of time. Strain into the container with the first batch of mushrooms.

Cover the mushrooms with olive oil until required. They will keep for several months in the fridge quite happily. They are good at room temperature with a juicy rare steak or eaten from a jar with a cocktail stick.

pineapple chutney

This is the perfect accompaniment to hammed duck legs cured in brine (see page 25) or other cooked meats.

serves 4 as an accompaniment

> 2 white onions, peeled and diced into small chunks
> 50ml olive oil
> 1 tsp brown mustard seeds, toasted
> salt and pepper
> 1 garlic clove, peeled and finely sliced
> 1 pineapple, peeled and cut into chunks
> 1 sprig of fresh rosemary
> 1 tbsp (floral) honey
> 100ml cider vinegar
> 120g light brown sugar
> 50g blanched almonds, toasted

In a saucepan, sweat off the onion in the olive oil for 10–15 minutes. Add the mustard seeds and season. Add the garlic, followed by the remainder of the ingredients, and stir.

Gently stew down for 1 hour or more until a jammy consistency. Adjust the acidity – adding a touch more sugar if necessary – and season accordingly.

blood orange curd

You can use blood orange curd on toast or to make a tart. I like to serve it, mixed with some double cream, with the rhubarb compote and ginger ice cream on page 54.

makes about 350–400ml

> about 4 blood oranges (you need 150ml juice and
>   grated zest of 2 oranges)
> 4 medium egg yolks
> 100g caster sugar
> 75g unsalted butter, softened

Put the orange juice, grated zest, egg yolks and sugar in a large bowl over a pan of boiling water, and whisk until thickened.

Slowly add the softened butter until fully whisked in. Set in the fridge until required. The curd will keep for a few weeks, covered, in the fridge.

braised topside with anchovy and onion

I adapted this from Elizabeth David's classic An Omelette and a Glass of Wine. *It is one of the easiest and tastiest recipes I know.*

serves 4–6

300g unsalted butter
6 white onions, peeled and cut thickly into half-moons
1–2 kg beef topside, cut into portion-sized steaks
salt and pepper
2–3 bay leaves

Flavourings
2–3 garlic cloves, peeled and crushed
1–2 tbsp red wine vinegar
6 tbsp olive oil
5–6 anchovy fillets, chopped up
2 dried red chillies (bird's eye chilli)
1 very large handful of fresh flat-leaf parsley

Take a solid casserole with a lid and rub all over the inside with butter. Then scatter in some of the onion. Season the beef and layer over the onions. Continue to layer beef, onion and seasoning. Throw in the bay leaves. Smear a sheet of greaseproof paper with more butter and place, butter-side down, on top of the meat and onion.

Preheat the oven to 140°C/275°F/gas mark 1. Place the lid on the pot and heat over a flame until it starts to sizzle. Transfer to the oven and leave for 2 hours or so, until the meat is very tender.

Place the rest of the ingredients – the flavourings – into a food processor and blitz to make a paste. Stir the paste into the meat and juices. Replace the lid and leave to infuse for 30 minutes.

Gently reheat, and serve with mash and something green.

loin of venison marinated in garlic, grilled pears and rosemary

By April-time I start to veer from the heavy braised dishes of winter and look to lighten things, using what is about. We still have pears around, and by grilling them and serving them alongside the robust venison, they tend to become more interesting, adding a sweetness to the dish. The watercress's peppery taste complements the venison and pears nicely, and nods to the new season's produce about to come in.

serves 4

salt and pepper
½ large bunch of fresh rosemary
1 loin of venison (boned out from the saddle)
3 Williams or Conference pears
extra virgin olive oil
2 bunches of watercress

Garlic confit
3 garlic bulbs, cut in half
1 sprig of fresh rosemary
duck fat or olive oil to cover

Make the garlic confit first. Put the garlic in a saucepan with the rosemary sprig and cover with the fat or oil. Simmer for 20–30 minutes or until tender. Allow to cool in the fat or oil.

Squeeze the cooled garlic confit from the skins into a bowl, and mix with salt, pepper and 1½ tsp of chopped rosemary. Rub this into the venison fillet and allow to mature at room temperature for 30 minutes or so.

Char-grill or barbecue the venison over the embers when the flames have died down, to medium rare, for 20 minutes or so. Allow the meat to rest, catching any juices.

Cut the pears in half lengthways, remove the cores and season with salt, pepper and a small amount of extra virgin olive oil. Grill the pears (cut-side down) to colour, turn over and continue grilling until soft but still holding their shape. Reserve in a warm place or, at the very least, at room temperature.

To serve the venison, slice the meat into 5mm slices and arrange on plates with the watercress and pears. Spoon over any meat juices and drizzle with some best-quality extra virgin olive oil. Garnish with fresh rosemary sprigs.

marinated brecon venison with wild garlic, st george's mushrooms and horseradish cream

Venison is one of the most majestic of beasts to look at and eat, and should be treated with great respect when preparing and cooking. It must be the star of the show and any accompaniment should not try to overshadow it. When sourcing your venison, ask the butcher for its liver – it's a real delicacy.

serves 8–10

1 small haunch of venison, left on the bone
salt and pepper
enough salted pork fat or lardo, thinly sliced, to cover the whole haunch
as many St George's mushrooms as you can pick
garlic cloves, peeled and sliced
olive oil
wild garlic leaves and flowers
horseradish cream sauce, to serve

Marinade
6 juniper berries, crushed
2–3 cloves, ground
1 tbsp coriander seeds, roughly ground
6 garlic cloves, peeled and crushed
2 bay leaves, crushed and roughly chopped
3–4 mixed peppercorns, crushed
1 tbsp fresh thyme leaves, roughly chopped
olive oil
200ml or so of red wine

Along the length of the venison, make shallow incisions about 1cm into the flesh. Mix the dry marinade ingredients together, then rub them all over and into the scores. Drizzle with oil and red wine. Transfer to a large stainless-steel roasting tin and cover with clingfilm, and allow the meat to marinate for a few hours or, ideally, overnight.

When ready to cook, preheat the oven to about 180°C/350°F/gas mark 4. Season the leg with salt, cover with the salted fat or lardo slices and cook as for lamb, depending on weight. The meat should ideally be served medium rare – so cook for roughly 10–15 minutes per 450g.

After the allotted time, check the internal temperature by inserting a skewer into the meat, leave for 20 seconds, then check that it's warm to hot. If not, return to the oven and check every 20 minutes or so.

In a frying pan, sauté off the St George's mushrooms with nothing more than a sliver of garlic and a drop of olive oil, until they colour. Season. Throw in the wild garlic leaves, which should be as fresh as possible (they lose their pungency rapidly once picked). Stir a few times and put to one side. Don't over-wilt the leaves and try to maintain some body.

Carve the meat and serve with warm horseradish cream sauce (*see* page 95) and any roasting juices. Scatter over the mushroom mixture and garnish with wild garlic flowers.

braised lamb or mutton breast

Another classic dish, using the breast of the sheep, a part of the animal that is often overlooked. It gives a delicious flavour and melting texture, with the added bonus of being one of the cheapest cuts available.

serves 4 as a starter

50g unsalted butter

25ml olive oil

1 half lamb breast, including the belly

salt and pepper

2 white onions, peeled and diced

2 carrots, diced

½ head of celery, diced

1 garlic bulb, cut in half

1 tbsp tomato purée

2–3 bay leaves

2–3 rosemary sprigs

200ml red wine

1 tbsp red wine vinegar

500ml water or lamb stock (*see* page 295)

caper mustard vinaigrette or tartare sauce, to serve

In a large saucepan melt the butter and olive oil together. Season the lamb breast generously and seal on all sides until golden. Remove from the pan.

Add the vegetables to the pan, including the garlic bulb, and sauté until golden, about 20–25 minutes. Stir in the tomato purée, herbs, red wine and red wine vinegar. Put the lamb breast back into the pan and cover with the stock or water.

Bring to the boil, cover and simmer for around 1½–2½ hours until tender. Remove the lamb carefully from the pan and place between two heavy baking trays to keep it flat. Refrigerate overnight.

The next day gently remove the bones from the meat and cut the flesh into fingers. These can either be reheated in the stock and eaten as is, or they can be dipped in flour, egg and breadcrumbs and deep-fried or oven-baked until golden. Serve with a caper mustard vinaigrette or tartare sauce (*see* opposite) and a bowl of seasonal leaves. The important thing here is to serve the lamb with something with a tartness that will cut through the fattiness of the meat.

caper mustard vinaigrette

Capers are a traditional match for mutton or lamb; they supply the necessary piquancy to balance the richness.

serves 4

1 tsp baby capers
1 tbsp sherry vinegar
3 tbsp olive oil
1 tsp Dijon mustard
½ garlic clove, peeled and crushed

Mix all the above ingredients together to make a vinaigrette. Serve with lamb or mutton.

tartare sauce

May sound a little strange to serve tartare sauce with meat, but the piquancy of the sauce works beautifully with the fatty richness of meat. This mayonnaise develops as it is left in the fridge. It will keep quite happily for a few days.

serves 4

Mayonnaise
3 medium egg yolks
1 garlic clove, peeled and crushed
1 tsp Dijon mustard
salt and pepper
200ml salad oil (half veg/half olive)
1 squeeze of lemon juice

Flavourings
1 tbsp baby capers
1 tbsp chopped gherkins or cornichons
1 tsp chopped fresh tarragon

Mayonnaise, in my opinion, must be made by hand, or it will always look shop-bought.

Whisk the egg yolks in a bowl. Mix in the crushed garlic, Dijon mustard with a pinch of salt and pepper, then very slowly glug the oil in. Watch out that the eggs take all the oil on and do not separate. If at any stage the eggs look greasy, then stop, add a squeeze of lemon juice, then continue. Whisk until the mayonnaise is thick and creamy.

Stir the baby capers and gherkins through at the end, along with the tarragon.

slow-poached salmon with balsamic vegetables

Use wild salmon if you can get it. There was an abundant supply in this area when I was a child, but we can rarely get hold of Usk or Wye salmon for the restaurant any more.

serves 4

1 litre olive oil
1 small bunch of fresh fennel tops or dill
2 star anise
½ tsp white peppercorns
½ tsp coriander seeds
4 salmon fillets, each about 175–200g in weight, rinsed
1 tbsp fresh marjoram or oregano leaves, to serve

Balsamic vegetables

8 pickling onions or shallots
8 small young carrots
8 small young leeks
8 celery sticks, from the inner part of the plant (reserve the leaves for garnish)
1 large fennel bulb, cut into quarters
100ml extra virgin olive oil
2 tbsp sherry vinegar
2 tbsp balsamic vinegar

Preheat the oven to 150°C/300°F/gas mark 2.

Ensure, for the purposes of even cooking, that all the vegetables are roughly the same thickness. If you cannot get young vegetables, then simply cut larger ones down to the same size (although they will lack much of the natural sweetness of the baby variety). In a large pan or roasting tin, fry off the vegetables in a little of the olive oil until they start to take on some colour. Pour in the two vinegars and swirl round the pan until rich and sticky. Pour in the remaining olive oil then roast the vegetables in the preheated oven for 10 minutes or so until just starting to soften. Allow to cool and marinate at room temperature for a few hours.

Meanwhile, to make the salmon, gently warm the olive oil with the aromatics until finger hot (not boiling, roughly 60°C/140°F). At this point, take the pan off the heat and put somewhere warm. Slip the salmon into the pan and allow it to poach slowly for 8–10 minutes, until it's still just pink in the middle. Remove the salmon, blot the excess oil off and keep somewhere warm.

Serve with the roasted balsamic vegetables either warm or at room temperature, never from the fridge. Scatter with the fresh herbs.

Note: The poaching oil can be strained and reused but be careful what you use it for, as it will have a fishy taste. Keep it in the fridge.

roasted hake with
ink-braised squid

A super-fresh piece of meaty white fish looks very dramatic and impressive sitting atop the inky black squid, but it's very easy to prepare. The dish can be garnished with a little gremolata, a mixture of finely chopped parsley, lemon zest and garlic.

serves 4

4 x 200g fillets freshest hake or cod, off the bone and rinsed
sea salt and pepper
olive oil

Ink-braised squid
3 white onions, peeled and diced
100g unsalted butter
2kg fresh large squid, cleaned and diced
2–3 bay leaves
a few sacs of fresh cuttlefish ink, or about 10 packets squid ink
  (it must be black, not grey)
500ml white wine

Gremolata
80g fresh parsley, finely chopped
finely chopped zest of 2 lemons
3 garlic cloves, peeled and finely chopped

Preheat the oven to 200°C/400°F/gas mark 6.

To start the squid, sweat the onion in the butter in a saucepan until translucent, then toss in the squid. Season with some sea salt, throw in the bay leaves and add the squid ink. Pour in the white wine, bring to the boil, reduce the heat, cover and leave to simmer for 1–2 hours. Once the squid is tender, leave to cool in the stock.

Season the fish, and then pan-fry it in some olive oil until golden on both sides, about 4–5 minutes. Place in the hot oven until cooked through, about another 5 minutes. While the fish is cooking, combine the gremolata ingredients.

Warm the squid in some of its cooking liquor until hot, then arrange on the plates with the hake on top. Serve with the gremolata on the side.

raoul's sea-beet with nutmeg and lemon sauce

Sea-beet or sea spinach can be collected even by the amateur forager along most stretches of British seashore. It has a waxy texture, a bit like a thick-leafed spinach, and holds its weight well when cooked. It has a deliciously herbal, salty tang. This is my great friend Raoul's way to use it.

serves 4 as an accompaniment

1kg sea-beet or sea spinach
salt and pepper
50g unsalted butter
30g plain flour
juice of 1 lemon
250ml milk, warmed
freshly grated nutmeg

Preheat the grill.

Wash the sea-beet. Briefly dip into a saucepan of boiling salted water for 1 minute until it just loses its shape. Remove from the pan, drain and lay in an ovenproof dish.

Melt the butter in a medium saucepan, add the flour and stir together to make a roux. Cook out for 5 minutes, then mix in the lemon juice and some salt. Pour the warm milk into the sauce gradually, stirring all the time, until the sauce thickens. Grate in nutmeg to taste.

Pour the sauce through a sieve and spoon over the sea-beet. Grill to colour, a few minutes only. Serve.

previous page *This is my great friend Raoul, both foraging expert and the only man I know who can carry off a hat like that!*

purple-sprouting broccoli with an anchovy and basil sauce

In my kitchen, anchovy has become a classic, and a necessary, salty accompaniment to one of the season's most notable vegetables. This anchovy sauce keeps well in the fridge and gets better with age. Serve with roast lamb or a suitably robust fish, like pollack or hake.

serves 4

360–400g purple sprouting broccoli
salt

Sauce
3 garlic cloves, peeled
1 small red chilli
1 x 50g can anchovy fillets, drained
3 tsp red wine vinegar
½ bunch of fresh basil, roughly chopped
6–8 tbsp extra virgin olive oil

Blanch the broccoli in a saucepan of boiling salted water for 2 minutes. Drain well.

Either blend all the sauce ingredients in a food processor, adding the olive oil slowly, or pound the ingredients in a pestle and mortar.

Spoon the sauce over the warm purple-sprouting broccoli, and serve.

st george's mushrooms, wild garlic and bacon

Just great country ingredients together on a plate. It's simple dishes like these that have given rural cooking such a big following.

serves 4

8 thick rashers of bacon, either streaky or back
50g unsalted butter
1 garlic clove, peeled and finely sliced
400g fresh St George's mushrooms
1 large handful of fresh, clean wild garlic leaves

In a frying pan, fry the bacon in the butter until crisp and coloured. Remove and keep warm. Throw the garlic slivers into the pan, sizzle for 1 minute until golden and then add the mushrooms. Sauté for 2–3 minutes until cooked.

Cut the bacon into edible slices (this dish is a fork job only), put into the pan and add the wild garlic leaves. Stir to wilt the leaves.

This dish would go well with a plate of freshly fried eggs.

horseradish cream sauce

This is a hot and piquant sauce to accompany the venison haunch, but it works equally well with beef, of course, or even salmon. A good spoonful of crème fraîche stirred in at the end adds a slight sour note.

serves 8–10 with the venison haunch (*see* page 80)
½ white onion, peeled and diced
1 garlic clove, peeled and crushed
25g unsalted butter
125ml dry white wine, or to taste
150ml chicken stock (*see* page 296)
500ml double cream
80g freshly grated horseradish
salt and pepper

In a saucepan, sweat the onion and garlic off in the butter until soft but not browned. Add the dry white wine and reduce by half. Add the stock and reduce by half again.

Add the cream and bring to the boil. Take off the heat, strain if desired and stir in the horseradish. Season and serve.

peanut butter parfait and caramel sauce

Ben, one of my chefs, showed me this recipe. I'm not a fan of peanut butter normally, but this is utterly delicious.

serves 6–8

165g caster sugar

12 medium egg yolks

220g chunky peanut butter

200g double cream

50ml dark rum

Caramel sauce

250g caster sugar

250ml pourable double cream

250ml semi-whipped double cream

In a heavy-based saucepan, boil the caster sugar with 6 tbsp water to the soft ball stage – 116°C/240°F. You will need a sugar thermometer for this to be accurate.

In the meantime, whisk the yolks up in a food processor until light and pale. When ready, pour the sugar syrup down the side of the food processor on to the eggs. The bowl will heat up at this point, so keep whisking until it cools.

Stir in the peanut butter. Whip up the double cream and fold this and the alcohol into the peanut mix. Freeze in a terrine mould for at least 24 hours.

To make the caramel sauce, heat the sugar up in a dry pan until it liquefies and goes golden brown. Stop the caramelization by pouring in the double cream, taking care not to spill any of this molten goo as it is incredibly hot.

Pour this into the semi-whipped cream and pass through a sieve.

Serve the parfait in slices with the warm caramel sauce.

caramelized oranges

I have coupled this with the rum baba (see page 102), but I often serve these with pannacotta, plus a splash more Cointreau over the top.

serves 4–6
10 oranges or blood oranges
250g caster sugar
1 tbsp Cointreau

Remove the peel from 4 of the oranges and cut into thin julienne. Bring to the boil in a saucepan of cold water to cover. Once up to the boil, remove from the heat and drain off the water. Replace with more cold water to cover and bring back to the boil. Repeat this process three times in total. Cook with 50g of the sugar in a little water to cover for 30 minutes or so, until the zest is soft and edible.

Peel and segment all the oranges, holding them over a bowl to catch any juices. Add the blanched peel.

Put the remaining sugar in a small saucepan and heat gently until it starts to caramelize and change colour. Then, just before it catches, add the Cointreau and the reserved juice to stop the caramel going any further. Reduce the juices to make the orange syrup.

Stir in the orange segments and blanched peel, and allow to steep for at least 2 hours, preferably overnight.

monmouth pudding

This is a traditional Welsh recipe from the part of Wales I now live in. It's very similar to one of my all-time favourites, the now sadly unfashionable queen of puddings. It also uses up the remaining red fruits I've frozen from the previous summer.

serves 4–6

450ml milk
finely grated zest of 1 lemon
2 tbsp caster sugar
25g salted butter
90g fresh breadcrumbs, toasted with a sprinkle of brown sugar
3 large egg yolks

Topping
150g frozen raspberries
½ x 370g jar raspberry jam, preferably home-made

Meringue
3 large egg whites
75g caster sugar

Preheat the oven to 150°C/300°F/gas mark 2.

In a saucepan, simmer the milk, lemon zest, sugar and butter together. Stir in the toasted breadcrumbs and leave to stand for 30 minutes.

Stir the egg yolks into the breadcrumb mixture, then pour into a suitable, ovenproof serving dish. Bake in the preheated oven for 25–30 minutes until just set. Remove from the oven. Put the oven temperature up to 180°C/350°F/gas mark 4.

Scatter the soft fruit over the top of the dish and spoon the jam over.

Whisk the egg whites until they form firm peaks. Fold in the sugar and whisk again until stiff. Spoon the meringue over the dish and put in the oven for 8–10 minutes, until golden. Serve warm.

rice pudding with vanilla pineapple

I know several folk who think it sacrilegious to put anything out of the ordinary into their rice pudding, but if you're into the idea, then fried pineapple is so much more interesting than a dollop of jam.

Serves 6

1 litre full-fat milk
1 vanilla pod, split lengthways
1 cinnamon stick
150g caster sugar
1 pinch of salt
250g pudding rice
6 medium egg yolks
500ml double cream
25g unsalted butter

Vanilla pineapple
1 extra sweet pineapple (Costa Rican are the best, in my opinion)
50g unsalted butter
caster sugar, to sprinkle
1 pinch of Chinese five-spice powder (optional)
the seeds of 1 vanilla pod, mixed with a splash of brandy or rum

In a saucepan, gently warm the milk with the vanilla pod and cinnamon stick. Bring to the boil and add half the sugar and the pinch of salt. Add the rice and stir for about 30–40 minutes until the rice just loses its bite – a bit like risotto although not so nutty to the bite.

Mix the yolks with the remaining sugar. Heat the cream in a separate pan and pour on to the eggs and sugar (as for crème anglaise), mixing well. Stir into the cooked rice and continue to stir for 1–2 minutes until thickened. Do not boil at this point. Stir in the butter and remove from the heat.

Meanwhile, peel and core the pineapple. Cut the flesh into batons. Melt the butter in a frying pan and lightly fry the pineapple with a sprinkling of sugar and five-spice powder, if using. Flip about to glaze and caramelize. Pour in the vanilla and alcohol mix. Simmer to cook the pineapple a little more.

Serve the rice pudding hot, with the hot pineapple.

treacle tart

This is one of my childhood favourites. I've incorporated a little grated apple into the filling, just to take the edge off the sweet syrup. The apple melts away when cooked, just leaving a slight sour note.

Serves 8

1 blind-baked 30cm pastry tart shell (*see* page 144)
1 pinch of freshly grated nutmeg
clotted cream or custard, to serve

Filling
500ml golden syrup
finely grated zest and juice of 1 lemon
150g brioche or croissant crumbs
250ml double cream
5 medium eggs, beaten
1 Bramley apple, peeled and grated

Preheat the oven to 170°C/325°F/gas mark 3.

Heat the syrup, lemon zest and juice together in a medium saucepan. Stir in the crumbs and the cream. When cool, add the eggs and the grated apple.

Pour into the pastry tart shell and bake in the preheated oven for between 30 and 40 minutes or until the tart is fully set and shows no sign of wobble. As soon as it comes out of the oven, sprinkle the nutmeg over. Allow to cool.

Serve warm or cold with clotted cream or custard.

rum baba

*I have very fond memories of eating rum babas, or 'savarins' as chefs like to call them,
in scary 1970s restaurants. This is my attempt to recreate that boozy, tooth-slaying treat.*

serves 6

500g self-raising flour
10g salt
caster sugar
20g fresh yeast
150ml water, warm
6 medium eggs, beaten
2 tsp milk, warmed
150g unsalted butter, softened
caramelized or fresh orange segments
  and Jersey cream, to serve

Grand Marnier sauce
200g caster sugar
300ml water
1 vanilla pod, split lengthways
3–5 tbsp Grand Marnier (or rum)
finely grated zest of 2 oranges

For the rum baba, sift the flour, salt and 40g caster sugar into a bowl. Crumble the yeast
into the warm water with a little more sugar. Stir the warm water and yeast into the
flour, and mix. Slowly stir in the eggs, warm milk and softened butter until you have
a smooth batter. When all has been brought together, cover the bowl with clingfilm and
allow to prove for at least an hour.

Knock back the soft dough and knead for 10 minutes until smooth and springy. The
dough should lose all of its cellulite appearance.

Butter a 20–25cm ring mould and spoon in the dough. Leave to rise for 15 minutes.

Preheat the oven to 180°C/350°F/gas mark 4.

Bake the rum baba for 30 minutes or so until the surface is golden and well risen, or
a knife inserted comes out cleanly. Allow to cool in the tin. (Or you can use individual
moulds if you'd prefer, and cook for about 15 minutes.)

Meanwhile, make the sauce. In a small saucepan, bring the caster sugar to the boil
with the water and vanilla pod. Boil only until the sugar has dissolved. Add the Grand
Marnier to taste, along with the orange zest. (During the winter months it is better done
with the bitter Seville oranges or blood oranges when in season.)

Finally, prick the baba all over, to better absorb the liquid. Place in a serving dish
and pour over the Grand Marnier sauce. Serve with some caramelized or fresh orange
segments and some very thick Jersey cream.

MAY • JUNE

MAY AND JUNE

As the year progresses, the need to be highly creative in the kitchen diminishes. Britain's farmers produce an array of delightful treats and, as a result, at this time of year hardly any effort is required to create the most exciting of menus.

The key ingredient for me is local asparagus – we are very lucky to have a neighbour who grows some of the best I've ever tasted. It's so popular locally, you can even buy it in our corner shop in Raglan. This is the only time of the year I don't mind repeating an ingredient on the menu – the first picking of this most prestigious of home-grown produce sends waves of excitement through my kitchen.

We now have four to six weeks to gorge on asparagus – steamed with grated Parmesan, tossed into a risotto primavera, smothered in béarnaise and, my favourite, covered with melted Taleggio cheese and the best Iberico ham. It all too soon departs again for another year, but no matter how desperate you are, don't be tempted by the imports. It makes it all the more special when spring comes round again.

It seems to me that ingredients often have a natural affinity with one another and this is never more evident than at this time of year. Jersey Royals partner beautifully with asparagus, as do young broad beans with fresh garden mint. A serving of wild Usk salmon would seem naked without some salty marsh samphire hand-picked from the Severn estuary.

We start seeing a lot of Raoul, our wild man of the woods, from this point on. He pops in through the winter with small amounts of sea-beet, sorrel and bitter cress, but as of now we can't get rid of him or his tall tales! His basket of goodies fills the kitchen with the scent of elderflowers, a fragrance sorely missed throughout winter, and he now starts bringing us such delights as hop shoots and chicken of the woods.

asparagus with hollandaise

Asparagus should always be used quickly, while it still gives a good 'snap' when bent in half. The stems should be young and not at all fibrous. During the blood orange season (January to March), this hollandaise, with 150ml juice added, goes well with purple sprouting broccoli.

serves 4

1 large bunch of best-quality fresh asparagus spears, ends cut or snapped
sea salt

Hollandaise
3 banana shallots, peeled and finely diced
1 sprig of fresh thyme
3 white peppercorns
1 bay leaf
1 splash of white wine vinegar
125ml white wine
3 large egg yolks
250g unsalted butter, melted until pourable
1 squeeze of lemon juice

To make the hollandaise, put the shallots, thyme, peppercorns and bay leaf into a small saucepan. Pour in the white wine vinegar and the white wine. Reduce until the liquid in the pan is barely a tablespoon.

Pull off to the side of the stove and, working quickly, whisk in the egg yolks. Keep whisking over a gentle heat over a pan of water, or at the side of the stove, until the yolks have doubled in volume and the eggs leave a ribbon-like trail. This will take 5 minutes or more of constant whisking.

Slowly pour in the melted butter until it's all incorporated into the eggs. Should the mixture split at this point, a small amount of hot water whisked into the side of the bowl should remedy the situation.

Now season with salt and lemon juice and then push through a sieve. The hollandaise should be a beautiful golden colour.

Throw the asparagus into a saucepan of rapidly boiling salted water and cook for no more than 2–3 minutes. Serve the asparagus very simply with a little flaked sea salt and a big dollop of the hollandaise.

local asparagus, taleggio cheese and iberico ham

The key to this very simple dish is the freshness of the asparagus – use only British and only when in season – and the supreme quality of the other ingredients.

serves 4

1 bunch of best-quality asparagus spears, ends cut or snapped
olive oil
4 slices of Taleggio cheese (or Emmental/Gruyère)
8 small slices of Iberico ham (or good-quality Parma ham)
freshly ground black pepper

Preheat the grill to the highest temperature.

Throw the asparagus, drizzled with some oil, under a hot grill (or on to a char-grill). Blacken slightly but don't overcook – the asparagus should still have some crunch.

Lay a slice of Taleggio cheese over each quarter-portion of the spears and put under the grill until the cheese turns golden and starts to bubble.

Plate up the asparagus and cheese and place the slices of ham over the top. Add freshly ground black pepper to taste. Serve immediately.

caesar salad with
deep-fried anchovies

Every chef and his dog does a version of Caesar salad and generally quite badly. This is one of the good ones!

serves 4

2 red endive or red romaine lettuce, separated into leaves
2 slices of white bread, sliced into croutons, and oven-baked with garlic and thyme oil
100g Parmesan, freshly grated
4 medium eggs, soft-boiled

Dressing
3 medium egg yolks
2 garlic cloves, peeled and crushed
1 tbsp Dijon mustard
salt and pepper
150ml each of olive oil and peanut oil
juice of ½ lemon
8–10 anchovy fillets
100g Parmesan, freshly grated

Deep-fried anchovies
2 handfuls, about 20–30, of fresh anchovies
milk
plain flour
vegetable oil, for deep-frying
smoked paprika, for dusting

In a mixer make the dressing as for mayonnaise (*see* page 85), but stirring in the Parmesan and anchovies at the end. Taste and season with salt and pepper.

For the deep-fried anchovies, dip the little fish in some milk then dust in flour. Heat the oil for deep-frying to 175°C/350°F (in a pot or wok) and deep-fry until golden brown. Remove, drain well, and throw some salt and smoked paprika at them. Keep warm.

To assemble the dish, dress the lettuce in a large bowl with the thick anchovy dressing. Throw in the croûtons and a good amount of grated Parmesan.

Pile on a plate and break the soft-boiled egg over the top. Scatter with the deep-fried anchovies and add a little more Parmesan. Serve.

risotto primavera

'Primavera' is Italian for spring, but literally translated, it means 'first green'. The point of a risotto or pasta primavera is making the most of the very first broad beans, fennel, asparagus, leeks, baby carrots and peas. It is a perfect British dish – because we do love our vegetable gardens – and this is the perfect way to use the best of the crop.

serves 4

8 young leeks, cleaned
8 young carrots
150g shelled broad beans
150g shelled fresh peas
8–10 small asparagus spears
salt and pepper
1.5 litres vegetable stock (*see* page 297)
a few Parmesan rinds
1 large white onion, peeled and finely diced

olive oil
100g unsalted butter
1 garlic clove, peeled and finely chopped
a few sprigs of fresh thyme, leaves picked
250g carnaroli or arborio risotto rice
125ml good-quality fruity white wine
1 tbsp mascarpone cheese
100g Parmesan, freshly grated
1 squeeze of lemon juice

Firstly, prepare the vegetables. Blanch the leeks, carrots, broad beans, peas and asparagus in a saucepan of boiling salted water, then refresh in iced water. Drain well and keep to one side. At this point have the vegetable stock boiling away in a saucepan, with the Parmesan rinds thrown in for flavour.

Sweat off the diced onion in a big splash of olive oil and 50g of the butter. Add the garlic clove and thyme. This should take about 10 minutes of slow cooking – do not colour the onion at all. Stir the rice into the onions and stir about for a few moments. When the rice is begging for liquid, throw in the white wine and the rice will now start sizzling. Keep stirring to evaporate the liquid. Then add the hot stock slowly, ladle by ladle, so that the rice incorporates each spoonful quickly. Stir throughout to prevent the rice from sticking and speed up the evaporation.

Continue doing this for about 15–20 minutes, until the rice is almost cooked and the stock is used up. Now throw in the vegetables and spoon in the mascarpone. Then add most of the Parmesan and season. Add the squeeze of lemon if some acidity is needed. A small knob of butter at this stage will add extra richness. Stir the risotto and add a touch more stock if required – the consistency should be a little loose.

Allow to rest in the pan for a few minutes to relax and absorb the rest of the liquid. Serve still quite wet with some more freshly grated Parmesan.

Note: Fresh herbs such as tarragon or chervil could be added at the end to lighten the risotto – and if the idea of blanching the vegetables bores you, throw them all in at the beginning of the dish when the onion is added. (The vegetables will lose some colour but the risotto will still be delicious!)

tuscan tomato soup

Traditional recipes always seem to be the best. This soup was a means of using up leftover bread and making the most of the abundant tomatoes and fabulous local olive oil. It's best made with the ripest tomatoes and the stalest bread, and good-quality olive oil. The bread should not sit in the soup long enough to become too pappy or the freshness is lost and the soup becomes stodgy. This should be a real summery treat.

serves 4–6

extra virgin olive oil
2 tsp chopped fresh sage leaves
4 garlic cloves, peeled and cut into slivers
10 fresh tomatoes, skinned and chopped
1 x 400g can plum tomatoes
4 x 2.5cm slices of stale ciabatta bread
salt and pepper
1 litre stock (vegetable or chicken, *see* pages 297 and 296)
1 bunch of fresh basil
freshly grated Parmesan

Heat up a big slug of olive oil in a saucepan, throw in the sage, garlic and the raw tomatoes and stir. Add the canned plum tomatoes and also the stale bread. Season.

Pour in the stock and simmer for 45 minutes. Stir frequently to break down and smooth out the soup.

Serve at room temperature topped with freshly torn basil, grated Parmesan and plenty of extra virgin olive oil.

ricotta, courgette and pea shoot salad, with yoghurt and lemon dressing

Fresh, light and healthy, and yet still worth eating...can't be right.

serves 4

1 lemon
2 yellow courgettes
2 green courgettes
salt and pepper
extra virgin olive oil
4 tbsp good-quality ricotta cheese
1 large handful of pea shoots
2 dessertspoons fresh shelled peas
a few sprigs of fresh mint

Yoghurt and lemon dressing
800ml Greek yoghurt
6 tsp runny honey
finely grated zest and juice of 2 lemons
2 tbsp chopped fresh mint

For the dressing, mix together the yoghurt, honey, lemon juice and zest, then throw in the freshly chopped mint.

Cut the zest off half the lemon and cut into needle threads. Keep to one side. Using a potato peeler, peel the courgettes lengthways into long strips. Put on to a plate and season with salt and pepper, some olive oil and a squeeze of lemon juice. Set aside.

Assemble the dish by mingling the cheese with the courgettes, pea shoots, peas and lemon zest. Drizzle with the yoghurt dressing and throw over the mint sprigs. Serve immediately.

rhubarb chutney

You may think this an unlikely partnership at first, but I recommend this chutney with grilled mackerel or salted pork.

fills 1 small Kilner jar

2 onions, peeled and sliced into half-moons

1 large knob of fresh root ginger, peeled and cut in half

50ml olive oil

1kg rhubarb, cut into chunks and washed

500g light brown sugar

200ml red wine vinegar

salt and pepper

Sweat off the onion and ginger in the olive oil in a heavy-based saucepan. Add the rhubarb, sugar and vinegar and stew down gently for about 1 hour until jammy in texture.

Season and serve.

slow-roast pork belly, gooseberry chutney and watercress

The peppery watercress and tart gooseberries go really well with the rich belly pork.

serves 4

1 whole pork belly (approx. 2kg)
salt
juice of 1 large lemon
1 large bunch of fresh watercress, to serve

Gooseberry chutney
2 large handfuls of fresh gooseberries
100ml white wine or cider vinegar
at least 200g caster sugar, to taste
1 tbsp chopped fresh rosemary
150ml gooseberry wine (if available), or medium to sweet white wine
2 tbsp mustard seeds, freshly toasted

Set the oven high to about 220°C/425°F/gas mark 7

Season the pork with salt and roast on a rack over a water bath for 30 minutes or so to start the crackling off. (The water stops the oven from filling with smoke from the dripping fat.) Turn the oven down to 160°C/325°F/gas mark 3, and roast slowly for an hour. Squeeze the lemon over the skin and continue to roast for a further hour, 2 hours in all. The lemon acid will help to crisp up the skin.

Remove the pork from the oven and allow to rest for 30 minutes. The meat should be meltingly tender. If the skin is still not crispy enough try blistering under a hot grill or cook the pork for a further 2 minutes at full whack.

For the chutney, simply throw all the ingredients into a saucepan and simmer until the gooseberries break down and the chutney starts to thicken. You want the chutney to be able to hold its own weight. Season to taste with salt and black pepper and some more caster sugar if necessary.

Serve thick slices of pork belly with the chutney and some fresh watercress.

duck with white onion, thyme and red wine risotto

This dish is great as it is, but it would be even better with the addition of other duck pieces – like livers, hearts or confit leg meat.

serves 4

2 large duck breasts

Risotto
500ml chicken or duck stock (*see* page 296)
2 white onions, peeled and finely diced
75g unsalted butter
salt and pepper
1 tbsp fresh thyme leaves
1 garlic clove, peeled and finely crushed
350g arborio or carnaroli risotto rice
150ml rich red wine
50g Parmesan, freshly grated
1 large tbsp mascarpone cheese

Preheat the oven to 180°C/350°F/gas mark 4.

Cook the duck breasts to your personal taste, but preferably pink, either on or off the bone. Gently fry in an ovenproof pan, skin-side down, for 5–6 minutes until golden, then roast in the preheated oven for a further 10–12 minutes. Allow to rest in a warm place and catch the juices that run from the meat.

Meanwhile, for the risotto, have the stock heating through in a saucepan. In a large saucepan, fry off the diced onion in most of the butter with a pinch of salt until soft, then add the thyme leaves and garlic. Stir in the rice and shuffle around the pan for a few minutes until the rice cries out for liquid. Add the red wine and sizzle to reduce. When nearly disappeared, add a ladle of hot stock and continue to do so until the stock has all gone and the rice is cooked 'to the bite'. This will take 20 minutes or so.

Finish off the risotto by stirring in the remaining butter, the Parmesan and mascarpone until everything is incorporated. Season.

Now slice the well-rested duck. Arrange over generous spoonfuls of the risotto on individual hot plates, making sure any meat juices are poured over the risotto.

braised beef short ribs with polenta crisps

Beef short ribs are tender and delicious when slow-cooked. They are rarely used in Britain, which is crazy because they are one of the tastiest cuts. For the restaurant, we buy them in as off-cuts from the trimmed ribs of beef, so you'll probably need to find a helpful local butcher.

serves 4

2 white onions, peeled and sliced
approx. 2kg beef ribs, cut into
  7.5cm pieces
½ bunch of fresh thyme
1 garlic bulb, cut in half
a few bay leaves
300ml white wine
50ml red wine vinegar
100ml rich chicken stock or dark
  veal stock (*see* pages 296 and 294)
salt and pepper

Polenta crisps

800ml fresh vegetable stock (*see* page 297)
1–2 pieces of Parmesan rind
1 sprig of fresh rosemary
1 garlic clove
200g quick-cook polenta, plus extra
  for coating
100ml double cream
2 medium eggs and 1 egg yolk
50g Parmesan, freshly grated
vegetable oil, for deep-frying
plain flour

Preheat the oven to 160°C/325°F/gas mark 3.

First start the polenta crisps. Bring the stock up to the boil in a deep and saucepan, add the Parmesan rinds, rosemary and garlic, and leave to infuse for 10 minutes. Strain, bring back to the boil, pour in the polenta and stir over a low heat until it thickens and comes away from the sides of the pan, about 5 minutes. Add the double cream, 1 of the egg yolks, beaten, and the grated Parmesan and stir well. Pour into a shallow tray lined with clingfilm and transfer to the fridge to set firm, for at least 2 hours.

For the short ribs, scatter the onion over the base of a heavy saucepan with a good-fitting lid. Throw in the ribs, thyme, garlic, bay leaves and all three liquids – wine, vinegar and stock. Season, cover and braise in the preheated low oven for 1½ hours. After this time, check the ribs and baste in the juices from the pan. Put back in the oven and continue basting with the sauce until they are tender and the sauce starts to go sticky.

To finish the polenta crisps, heat the oil for deep-frying to 180°C/350°F (in a pot or wok). Remove the set polenta from the tray and cut into chunky diamonds. Put the flour on one plate, the remaining beaten eggs on another and the loose polenta on a third. Flour, egg and polenta each polenta diamond, then deep-fry until golden. Drain well.

Serve the melting ribs with the onion and sauce, along with the hot polenta crisps and a summer leaf salad, made with a selection of hot-house British lettuce and baby gems, radishes and cucumber, tossed in a dressing of crème fraîche, olive oil and seasoning.

rack of lamb with baby gem lettuce, peas, mint and bacon

I don't really need to comment much on this one, it's heavenly early summer on a plate.

serves 4

olive oil

2 x 8-bone racks of lamb

salt and pepper

4 sprigs of fresh thyme, leaves picked

4 medium baby gem lettuces, halved

75g unsalted butter

200g sliced pancetta or bacon

4 garlic cloves, peeled and thinly sliced

100g fresh shelled peas, blanched and refreshed

800ml lamb stock (*see* page 295)

4 sprigs of fresh mint, leaves picked and torn, plus extra to garnish

Preheat the oven to 200°C/400°F/gas mark 6.

Heat 1tbsp olive oil in a large heavy-based frying pan. Season the lamb fat with salt and pepper, then fry fat-side downwards for a few minutes over a high heat until browned. Turn over, put into a roasting tin, and sprinkle with some of the fresh thyme. Roast in the preheated oven for 15–20 minutes or to your liking. Leave to rest for 10 minutes before serving.

In another frying pan, colour off the baby gem lettuce, cut-side down, in 15g of foaming butter. Throw in the diced pancetta, the garlic and remaining thyme, and sauté off for a few minutes until coloured. Add the peas and pour in the lamb stock. Bring to the boil and simmer for 2–3 minutes to warm everything through.

Just before serving, cut the lamb into chops and place in a large serving bowl.

Throw the mint into the simmering stock along with the remaining butter. Stir in to enrich the sauce and give it a good sheen. Season carefully, as the pancetta or bacon may already have seasoned the stock sufficiently. Spoon around the lamb racks and serve garnished with extra mint.

spinach and ricotta flan

I don't usually do vegetarian, but this is an Italian recipe I discovered while holidaying in Florence, and I really love it.

serves 6–8 as a starter

unsalted butter, for greasing
1kg fresh spinach
salt and pepper
250g ricotta cheese
2 medium eggs
100g Parmesan, freshly grated
freshly grated nutmeg
70ml extra virgin olive oil

Preheat the oven to 160°C/325°F/gas mark 3, and grease a medium, about 20cm, spring-form flan tin.

Quickly blanch the spinach in a saucepan of boiling salted water. Drain, squeeze it dry and chop quite finely.

In a bowl stir all the ingredients together and season. Using a stick blender or food processor blitz the ingredients together. You should now have a green pulp that slightly resembles baby food.

Pour the mixture into the prepared tin and bake in the preheated oven for 5 minutes until crisp looking. Turn the temperature down to 100°C/210°F/a very low gas, and continue to cook for another 30–40 minutes. Remove and leave to cool a little.

Serve warm or at room temperature with some really good mozzarella and roasted cherry tomatoes, or melt some Gorgonzola over. Add some rocket and toasted pine nuts for that 1980s touch!

sewin, welsh cockles and soused vegetables

Now is a good time of year to sample sewin or sea trout. The flesh of the fish is a wonderful pink. It is quite a bit paler than salmon but can be cooked in pretty much the same ways – except that any accompanying sauce should be really delicate, as the fish has a light, distinctive flavour. Sousing is a simple way to accentuate the flavours of an exceptionally fresh fish.

serves 4

4 x sewin fillets, rinsed

400g cockles, scrubbed and rinsed

100g wild sorrel and 50ml extra virgin olive oil, to garnish

Poaching liquor

4 celery sticks

2 large onions, peeled

4 carrots

2 bay leaves

1 tsp black peppercorns

1 tsp coriander seeds

400ml white wine

200ml white wine vinegar

100ml water

First make the poaching liquor. Cut all the vegetables, on an angle, to the same thickness. Throw in a saucepan with all the remaining ingredients. Bring to the boil and simmer for 30 minutes. Remove from the heat.

Slip the sewin pieces into the poaching liquor and cook gently for 6–7 minutes. Do not allow to boil. Remove the fish and keep warm.

Put some of the cooking liquor in a small saucepan, bring to the boil and throw in the cockles. Add a lid and shake the pan from time to time. They should take 2–3 minutes to open. Remove the cockles from the heat and discard any that have not opened. Shell some of them, keeping some in the shell as garnish.

To serve, place some soused vegetables on to a warm plate, put a piece of sewin on top and scatter some cockles around the plate. Garnish with the wood sorrel, a splash of extra virgin olive oil and the in-shell cockles.

wild salmon 'en papillote' with clams, white wine and cucumber

Steaming or poaching a fresh, wild fish accentuates its quality and ensures that the clean, fresh flavours are retained, so avoid the harshness of roasting or frying. This technique is perfect for any delicate fish fillet, as shown opposite.

serves 2

½ cucumber, quite finely sliced
2 x 230g pieces wild salmon, rinsed
500g cockles or clams, in shell
salt and pepper
1 sprig of fresh thyme
1 bay leaf
25ml dry white wine
1 good splash of extra virgin olive oil.

Take a large dinner plate and use as a template to cut a circle of greaseproof paper. Fold this in half and open out again.

Lay the cucumber slices on one-half of the paper and put the fish on top, skin-side up. Scatter over as many cockles or clams as the bag can hold, then season, and carefully add the herbs, white wine and olive oil. Fold the paper over the fish and shellfish, and crimp along the edges.

Place on a baking sheet and bake in the preheated hot oven for 10 minutes or so until the salmon is cooked and the clams have opened.

Open the bag and check the fish. A sharp knife should run through the fish easily and the shellfish should be open. Discard any shells that do not open when the fish is cooked. This would accompany some warm buttered new potatoes and one of a thousand floppy-leaf salads, very well indeed.

overleaf *Steve Gill, fly-fishing and countryside supremo, giving me a lesson on which fly to use for that morning's catch.*

wild salmon with samphire and crayfish sauce

I like to put together ingredients that have a natural affinity, so salmon and crayfish together on a plate make sense to me. I also like to use crayfish whenever I can to do my bit to reduce their invasion of British rivers.

serves 4

4 fillets wild salmon, skin on, about 175–225g each, rinsed
sea salt and pepper
olive oil
100g or so fresh samphire, picked over but raw

samphire and crayfish sauce
1kg live crayfish
1 white onion, peeled and diced
1 garlic clove, cut in half

2 sprigs of fresh tarragon
15g fresh thyme leaves
10g fennel seeds
2 bay leaves
50g unsalted butter
125ml Martini or Noilly Prat
1 litre fresh fish stock (*see page 294*)
250ml double cream
1 pinch of smoked paprika
juice of 1 lemon

Kill the crayfish by dropping them into a saucepan of boiling water for 2 minutes. Remove and refresh in cold water. Separate the body from the head and remove the tail meat. Set the meat aside and keep all the shells.

To make the sauce, sweat off the onion and aromatics in half the butter. Add the alcohol when the onions are translucent and boil to reduce by half. Throw in the crayfish heads, claws and tail shells. Crunch up and stir to extract maximum flavour. Cover with the fish stock and simmer for 20 minutes or until reduced by half. Add the double cream, bring to the boil, and season with salt, paprika and lemon juice. Strain and reserve.

To cook the salmon, score the fillets, skin-side up, three times to prevent curling in the pan. Season the skin side with sea salt. Warm a pan, put in a splash of oil and pan-fry three-quarters of the way on the skin side, turn over and continue to cook until slightly pink in the middle (5–6 minutes depending on thickness). Remove and keep warm.

Wipe out the pan and throw in the samphire with the remaining butter. Season lightly and sauté for 3 minutes or so until cooked. Throw in the crayfish tail meat and sauté off for another minute. To serve, pile up the samphire and crayfish tails, put the wild salmon on top and spoon around the warmed crayfish sauce.

Note: For larger gatherings, put a whole side of salmon (ours weighed 1.25kg) on a sheet of non-stick baking paper set on a piece of foil, sprinkle with some chopped tarragon, a little chopped onion, a few fennel seeds, a few sprigs of fresh thyme, salt and black pepper. Dot with butter, juice from 1 lemon, cut into wedges, and a splash of Noilly Prat. Bake uncovered at 200°C/400°F/gas mark 6 for about 30 minutes. To check, press the centre of the salmon with a knife, the flakes should be an even colour all the way through; if not cook for a few more minutes and then re-test.

grilled mackerel with choucroûte, bacon and mustard sauce

Don't be scared of choucroûte, it has a beautifully delicate sour flavour, which goes perfectly with bacon and is ideal to balance the richness of the mackerel.

serves 4

**4 mackerel, left whole, gutted,
  heads removed, fins off, rinsed**
salt and pepper
lemon juice
olive oil

Choucroûte and bacon
**100g pancetta or smoked
  bacon, diced**
1 tbsp duck fat
1 garlic clove, peeled and crushed
a few springs of fresh thyme
2 bay leaves
a few juniper berries

500g choucroûte
1 bottle lager
1 tbsp finely chopped fresh parsley

Mustard sauce
**1 banana shallot, peeled and finely
  chopped**
25g unsalted butter
1 tbsp white wine vinegar
125ml white wine
100ml double cream
1 tsp coarse-grain mustard
1 tsp Dijon mustard

Preheat the grill to the highest temperature.

Fry off the pancetta in the duck fat until coloured. Add the garlic, thyme, bay leaves and juniper berries, sauté for a few minutes and then add the choucroûte. Pour in the lager, reduce and simmer the choucroûte for 10 minutes or so. Season carefully. Stir in the chopped parsley.

Meanwhile, make the mustard sauce. Sweat down the shallot in the butter until soft in a saucepan, then add the white wine vinegar and reduce. Add the white wine and reduce by half. Add the double cream and bring to the boil. Stir in the mustards and season to taste.

Season the mackerel with salt, pepper, lemon juice and olive oil, and grill until blistered and cooked through, about 8–10 minutes, depending on size.

Serve the fish with some choucroûte, and the sauce spooned around the choucroûte.

strawberries, oranges, cava and mint

This would make a refreshing end to a summer lunch. Feel free to use prosecco or champagne if you want to be extravagant...

serves 4

3 punnets fresh strawberries
1 tbsp caster sugar
½ vanilla pod, split lengthways
2 punnets wild strawberries (if available)
2 oranges, peeled and segmented
1 cucumber, deseeded and diced
2 bunches of white currants
2 bunches of redcurrants
1 bunch of fresh mint, roughly torn
1 x 750ml bottle cava

Take 1 punnet of the large strawberries and purée with the caster sugar and vanilla seeds. Sieve the sauce. Taste and add more sugar if necessary.

Pour some of the strawberry sauce into the bottom of 4 serving dishes. Arrange the rest of the fruit on top of the purée and scatter over the mint.

Pour the cava over each bowl of fruit at the table and allow to fizz about. Serve immediately.

poached cherry pavlova, vanilla cream and toasted pistachios

I love the combination of sweet and sour in this pudding, and the sprinkling of pistachios adds an unexpected sweet crunchiness at the end of each mouthful.

serves 4–6

50g shelled pistachio nuts
2 tbsp icing sugar
300ml double cream
1 vanilla pod, split lengthways

Cherries in stock syrup
200ml water
125g caster sugar
pared zest of ½ orange
1 cinnamon stick, halved
400g fresh cherries
1 splash of Kirsch

Pavlova
4 medium egg whites
225g caster sugar
1 tsp cornflour
½ tsp vanilla extract
1 tsp white wine vinegar
75g dried sour cherries,
  roughly chopped

Preheat the oven to 130°C/260°F/gas mark ½. For the cherry stock syrup, put all the ingredients except for the cherries and Kirsch in a non-reactive pan, and cook until the sugar has just dissolved. Remove stones and stalks from two-thirds of the cherries, then poach all the cherries in the sugar syrup until just tender, about 10 minutes or so. Add a big splash of Kirsch to this, if liked.

Toast the pistachio nuts with the icing sugar in a non-stick pan, then tip out on to a piece of non-stick baking paper and leave to cool before roughly chopping. Reserve. Remove the cherries from the stove and allow to cool in the liquid. While they are cooling, take a ladle of the poaching liquid and reduce to a semi-sticky syrup consistency. This will decorate the dish when serving and add depth of flavour.

To make the pavlova, in a mixer whisk up the egg whites and sugar to stiff peaks and until the sugar dissolves. This will take anywhere between 20 and 30 minutes, or until the sugar has completely dissolved. Throw in a mix of the cornflour, vanilla and white wine vinegar, and fold together with the dried sour cherries. Dollop or pipe the pavlova mixture on to non-stick baking sheets in individual portion sizes – they will expand, so about 1tbsp size per person. Cook in the preheated very low oven for 1–1½ hours, or until they lift off the non-stick sheet cleanly.

While the pavlova is cooking, whip the double cream with the scraped seeds of the vanilla pod and a splash of the Kirsch. Whip up to semi-stiff peaks – just until it holds its own weight. Set aside. To serve, spoon a generous amount of the vanilla cream on to each pavlova and drizzle over the stoned poached cherries and the reduced sauce. Scatter over some toasted pistachio nuts and decorate with cherries with stalks still on.

elderflower fritters with yoghurt and lime

I like to pick elderflower with the kids, then they help me make the batter for this dish. The fritters are very light and look pretty on the plate. They like theirs with ice-cream, but I prefer the texture and zestiness of this yoghurt.

serves 3–4

6–8 elderflower heads on stalks
fine white flour
4 tbsp caster sugar
vegetable oil, for deep-frying

Yoghurt
300g Greek yoghurt
1 tbsp icing sugar
finely grated zest and juice of 1 lime
seeds from ½ vanilla pod

Batter
450g fine white flour
1 x 330ml bottle lager
25g fresh yeast
enough sparkling water to make a slack paste (500ml)

Mix all the yoghurt ingredients together in a bowl and reserve. For the batter, mix the flour, beer and yeast together in a mixing bowl until smooth, then add enough sparkling water to make a slack paste.

Pick over the inside of the elderflower heads to remove any insects. Lightly flour, then dip into the batter. Heat the oil for deep-frying to 175°C/350°F and deep-fry for 2–3 minutes until golden. Drain well on kitchen paper.

Sprinkle with caster sugar and serve immediately with the lime yoghurt.

Note: You can deep-fry courgette flowers in exactly the same way. They make a fantastic savoury starter, accompanied by lemon wedges and grated Parmesan.

elderflower cordial

You can dilute it with water for a really refreshing summer drink or add a shot or two of gin, if you feel so inclined. I use the cordial to make jellies, granitas and elderflower posset or fool. It can also be used to sweeten the fruit in other seasonal puddings.

makes about 1.2 litres

12 elderflower heads
900g caster or granulated sugar
600ml water
2 lemons

Wash the elderflower heads gently and pick over to check for bugs, then place in a large bowl.

Put the sugar and water into a pan and bring to the boil, stir and simmer to completely dissolve the sugar.

Meanwhile, take the lemon zest off in thick strips and place in with the elderflowers. Then add the rest of the lemons, cut into slices. Pour the boiling syrup over the lemon and flowers, cover and leave overnight.

The next day, strain the cordial through a sieve lined with a clean kitchen cloth and pour the cordial into a thoroughly cleaned bottle for storage.

gooseberry crumble tart

It is a shame that they are not more popular as the British climate is particularly suited to producing perfect berries – juicy, very tart and full of flavour. At the start of the season, they are at their best for cooking. This is another inspired by my old boss, Alastair Little.

serves 12

600g fresh gooseberries
150ml sweet dessert wine
125g caster sugar, or more to taste
1 vanilla pod, split lengthways
pared zest of 1 orange
a few fresh elderflower heads,
  if in season, or a good dose of
  elderflower cordial, say 200ml

Crumble topping
50g blanched almonds
60g Italian 00 plain flour
1 pinch of salt

40g quick-cook polenta
50g caster sugar
2 drops vanilla extract
75g chilled unsalted butter, chopped

Pastry
280g plain flour
1 pinch of salt
230g unsalted butter, softened
2 medium egg yolks
1 vanilla pod, split lengthways
115g icing sugar
finely grated zest of 1 lemon (optional)

Preheat the oven to 180°C/350°F/gas mark 4. Top and tail the gooseberries and rinse. Put the sweet wine, sugar, vanilla pod and scraped seeds, orange zest and elderflower in a pan and bring to the boil. Leave to infuse for a few minutes, then add the gooseberries. Cover with a lid, pull off the stove and let sit in the hot liquid until soft. This will ensure the gooseberries do not explode when cooking.

To make the crumble, toast off the almonds, chop finely and mix with the flour, salt, polenta, sugar and vanilla. Rub in the butter and spread out over a baking sheet. Chill for 30 minutes to firm up. Bake in the preheated oven for 30–40 minutes. Remove and allow to cool. Break up with your hands. Set aside.

Meanwhile, to make the pastry, mix the flour and salt together. Make a well in the centre and add the soft butter, egg yolks, vanilla seeds, the icing sugar and lemon zest, if using. Combine, then roll into a log shape and wrap. Chill for at least an hour.

Remove the pastry from the fridge and dust a 30cm tart tin with extra flour. Cut the log of pastry into 1cm circles and arrange in the tart case – butting the edges of the circles together and pressing the edges to seal. (As the pastry is sugary, this keeps it short and prevents over-rolling.) Chill for 10 minutes. Blind-bake the tart shell (with the flan tin lined with greaseproof and baking beans) in the preheated oven, at the same temperature as above, until golden brown.

Drain off the gooseberries and fill the tart shell. Sprinkle over the crumble mix and reheat the whole tart for 10–15 minutes at 150°C/300°F/gas mark 2. Serve with fresh cream or good-quality ice-cream.

JULY ● AUGUST

JULY AND AUGUST

The British summer is now in full swing and superb locally grown produce always proves to be so much more satisfying than any foreign imports. This is one of those few times of the year when great home-grown food is always so easy to find – so it seems absurd that the supermarket shelves are full of foodstuffs from the other side of the world.

Strawberries, justifiably, must take centre stage – we can get some of the best from neighbouring Herefordshire, but there are a couple of super fruit farms almost within walking distance of the restaurant. I am always hopeful and have fingers crossed that, with some good sunshine, home-grown tomatoes can be almost as good as the Italian.

During these months, dining should be lazy and convivial, food should be simply prepared and relaxed in style. Above all, this is a time to enjoy good company and linger over simple, elegant dishes. There's no need to be out to impress. You should definitely make the most of the summer's fine coastal shellfish and celebrate it with plenty of chilled, crisp white wine...well, that's what I try to do anyway.

salt cod, poached duck egg and aïoli

This is best served warm or at room temperature. Essentially it is a pared-down 'Le grand aïoli'.

serves 4

1 thick fillet of cod, no less than 1kg, rinsed
sea salt
extra virgin olive oil
6 baby globe artichokes, cut in half and blanched for 10–12 minutes
150g best-quality black or green olives
4 duck eggs, poached for 6–7 minutes until just set
flat-leaf parsley and lemon wedges, to serve

Aïoli
3 garlic cloves, peeled and finely crushed
2 medium eggs
salt and white pepper
250ml extra virgin olive oil
juice of 1 lemon

Put the cod in a dish and cover with a heavy seasoning of sea salt. Cover and leave overnight in the fridge.

Preheat the oven to 180°C/350°F/gas mark 4.

To make the aïoli, put the crushed garlic in a bowl with the eggs and some salt and white pepper. Start to whisk, gradually adding the olive oil. Whisk until all the oil is in and the sauce is thick. Let it down with enough lemon juice to taste. Reserve.

Quickly rinse off the salted cod fillet and pat dry.

Heat a non-stick frying pan. Add some oil and pan-fry the cod, flesh-side down, until golden brown, 3–4 minutes. Turn the fish over and put into the preheated oven until cooked through, about 5 minutes. Test with the point of a knife – if it goes in without resistance it's ready. Keep the fish somewhere warm.

Toss the well-drained artichokes and olives in some good oil, and season.

To assemble the dish, lay the fish flesh-side up, top with a cracked poached egg, aïoli on the side and artichokes and olives scattered over. Garnish with flat-leaf parsley and a lemon wedge.

tuna with runner beans, pine nuts and raisins

Don't be scared of serving the tuna a little rare. The salad is best served at room temperature or just warm.

serves 2

10 blanched almonds
1 bunch each of fresh parsley, mint and marjoram, chopped
2 tuna steaks, about 230g each
50ml freshly squeezed orange juice
1 tsp lemon juice
100ml dry white wine
20g raisins, soaked in hot water then drained
30g pine nuts, toasted
200g runner beans, blanched and finely sliced

Make a paste from the almonds and herbs using a food processor.

In a hot, nonstick frying pan, sear the tuna on both sides for 1–2 minutes. Remove from the pan and keep warm.

Deglaze the tuna pan with the citrus juices and white wine, and reduce by half. Add the herb paste, followed by the raisins and pine nuts. Stir in the runner beans and heat through for a few moments.

Throw a pile of the bean salad on to a plate and slice the tuna thickly over the top.

deep-fried sand eels or sprats

When we set up the restaurant some six years ago, sand eels were available in abundance. They looked beautiful when they arrived into the kitchen, all bright eyes and silver skin and tasted deliciously salty. Unfortunately, they are now, for one reason or another, extremely difficult to get hold of, but the common sprat works equally well.

serves 4

2 large handfuls of the chosen fish, approx. 120g per person, rinsed
salt and pepper
vegetable oil, for deep-frying
milk, for dipping
plain flour, for dusting

Take the heads off the fish and squeeze the guts out (these will taste bitter if left in). The best way then to clean the fish is to vigorously shuffle them about in heavily salted water. The abrasive action of the salt and water will help remove any remaining blood and guts. Pat the fish dry and refrigerate before using.

To fry the fish, heat the hot oil to 170°C/338°F or thereabout, but it must be hot before frying. When ready to fry, dip the fish alternately in some milk and seasoned flour, and fry in small batches to keep the oil temperature high. After a few minutes when the fish are turning golden brown, drain and serve immediately before they steam and go soggy.

Serve with various dips and some good salad leaves.

coriander and soured cream dip

This makes a great dip for crudités, and if thinned out with a little milk could also be drizzled over barbecued lamb.

serves 2

1 tbsp coriander seeds
1 garlic clove, peeled and crushed
juice of 1 lime
250g soured cream
1 tbsp chopped fresh coriander
salt and pepper

Toast off the coriander seeds in a dry pan for a few minutes. Crush in a pestle and mortar with the garlic clove. Squeeze in the lime juice and stir into the soured cream with the chopped coriander. Season to taste.

wasabi and soy dressing

I often use this as an accompaniment to seared salmon or tuna.

serves 4

2 tbsp wasabi powder
4 tbsp dark soy sauce
½ tbsp sesame seeds, toasted
1 tbsp sesame oil
juice of 1 lemon
1 splash of water
fresh red chilli (optional)

Simply mix all the ingredients in a bowl until the wasabi powder has dissolved in the soy and thickened. Add a little chopped red chilli, if desired.

potted crab

A variation on this dish, which I like just as well, is to add a little fresh chopped chilli and fresh coriander, and to substitute lime for the lemon.

serves 4

250g unsalted butter
450g pre-cooked mixed white and brown crabmeat
salt
1 scant pinch of freshly ground white pepper
juice of 1 lemon
1 tsp each of chopped fresh chervil and chives
2 tsp chopped fresh curly parsley
1 pinch each of cayenne pepper, ground mace and freshly grated nutmeg

Clarify the butter by warming gently in a saucepan on the side of a stove until the milk solids separate from the fat. Strain through a muslin and reserve just the molten butter.

Pick through the crabmeat, discarding any bone or shell. Season with salt, pepper, the lemon juice and soft herbs. Pack the crabmeat mix into 1 large or 4 small pots.

Stir the ground spices through the clarified butter and pour on to the crab pots. Chill until set. Serve with hot brown toast and a warm broccoli salad.

crab and samphire frittata with brown meat dressing

The trick with this recipe is to leave the middle just slightly runny. Overcooking, just as with an omelette, kills the dish.

serves 2

100g pre-cooked brown crabmeat
1 tbsp crème fraîche
salt and pepper
juice of 1 lemon
full-fat milk, to thin the sauce
40g freshly picked samphire
100g pre-cooked white crabmeat
100g each of chopped fresh chervil, dill and chives
6 medium eggs
olive oil

Preheat the grill to the highest temperature.

To make the brown crabmeat dressing put the meat in a mixer, add the crème fraîche, some salt and pepper and half of the lemon juice. Sieve the sauce and let it down with some full-fat milk until you have a sauce-like consistency. Reserve.

Blanch the samphire in a saucepan of boiling water. Remove and refresh in cold water. Reserve. Mix the white crabmeat with the fresh herbs and some salt, pepper and the remaining lemon juice.

To make the frittata, crack and beat the eggs lightly in a bowl and season. Drop into a small warm, lightly oiled frying pan. Pull the eggs away from the side. Put the white crabmeat mix in the middle. Top with the samphire and shuffle the mix about to mingle with the egg. Place under a hot grill to 'soufflé' a little and cook the eggs.

Serve on a big white plate with the brown crabmeat dressing around.

cockle and broad bean salad with herb vinaigrette

This is the sort of easy quick-cook dish that is called for during the summer: simple ingredients, cooked quickly. Best eaten with your fingers as a small starter or snack.

serves 4–6

1kg cockles, scrubbed and rinsed
125ml dry white wine
500g podded fresh broad beans

Herb vinaigrette
1 tbsp sherry vinegar
3 tbsp best-quality extra virgin olive oil
1 pinch of salt
½ garlic clove, peeled and crushed
1 tsp each of finely chopped fresh dill, chervil
  and chives

To make the vinaigrette, mix together the vinegar, oil, salt and garlic in a bowl. Stir in the herbs just before serving.

Put the cockles over a high heat in a dry saucepan. When the cockles hit the bottom of the pan throw in the white wine. Put a lid on and leave for a couple of minutes. Shake the pan to agitate the cockles. As soon as they begin to open stir for another minute, then drain in a colander, reserving both the liquor and cockle meat with it. Discard the shells, and any cockles that do not open.

Cook the broad beans for 3–4 minutes in a saucepan of boiling water. Drain and take off the outer skin if you have the time and inclination. Young broad beans don't need to be skinned.

Mix the broad beans with the cockle meat, dress in herb vinaigrette and serve.

lobster rice

You can use a more regular risotto rice, instead of wild rice, if you prefer, and different types of shellfish work just as well.

serves 4 as a starter, 2 as a main course

2 white onions, peeled and chopped

1 garlic clove, peeled and crushed

150ml olive oil

75g wild rice, cooked until split

1.5kg winkles, in shell (optional)

1.5g cockles, in shell

125ml dry white wine

1 pinch of saffron strands

1.5kg cooked lobster, at room temperature

salt and pepper

1 handful of flat-leaf parsley, roughly chopped

In a saucepan, sweat the onion and garlic in 100ml of the olive oil for 10 minutes. Stir in the cooked wild rice and set aside.

In a separate pan, cook the winkles (if using) and cockles in the white wine until open. Discard any that do not open. Drain in a colander and keep the juices.

Pick the meat from the shellfish, using a pin. Strain the juices from the shellfish into the rice mixture and reduce, stirring frequently.

Add the pinch of saffron and stir in chunks of the lobster meat and the shellfish. Taste, season and stir in the parsley. Drizzle the remaining olive oil over the rice when serving.

smoked salmon pizza

Once you get the hang of these thin crisp-based pizzas, you can experiment with all sorts of toppings. They are intentionally thin so that the focus is on the flavours and textures on top, not on a thick, doughy base.

makes 2 large pizzas, to serve 2–4

Pizza dough
900g Italian 00 plain flour
550ml water
25g fresh yeast
15g salt

Pizza topping
500g San Marzano tomatoes, finely diced
20g fresh oregano leaves
salt and pepper
extra virgin olive oil
4 tbsp soured cream
150g smoked salmon
10g fresh dill sprigs, or a herb of your choice, to garnish

To make the pizza dough, mix 550g of the flour, the water and fresh yeast together in a bowl to make a sponge. Cover with clingfilm and leave to rise for 1 hour.

Add the remaining flour and the salt, then mix and knead well. Roll into two balls and allow to rise on a lightly floured baking sheet in the fridge for half an hour. If you want to make smaller pizzas, you can: any remaining dough will freeze well.

Preheat the oven to its highest possible heat.

Roll out each pizza base until quite thin. Scatter over the diced tomatoes and oregano, season lightly and drizzle over the olive oil. Bake in the preheated oven until the dough is risen and slightly charred on the edges.

Remove, dot with the soured cream and lay the salmon over. Flash back through the oven for 30 seconds to take the chill off the salmon. Remove and scatter over the dill sprigs. Serve immediately.

wild sea bass, smoked paprika and braised white beans

Piquillo peppers, rocket and smoked paprika make a spicy accompaniment to these crisp fillets of sea bass.

serves 2

2 wild sea bass fillets, rinsed, trimmed and skin scored
best-quality extra virgin olive oil
salt and pepper
1 knob of butter
juice of 1 lemon

Beans
250g dried cannellini beans, soaked in cold water overnight
1 sprig of fresh rosemary
1 fresh red chilli
2 bay leaves
1 onion, peeled and quartered
1 carrot, peeled
1 celery stick
1 pinch of smoked paprika
100g piquillo peppers, diced
1 handful of rocket leaves
juice of ½ lemon

Drain the soaking beans and transfer to a large saucepan. Add the rosemary, red chilli, bay leaves, onion, carrot and celery. Pour over enough water to cover by 3cm. Bring to the boil and simmer for approximately 1½ hours or until the beans are soft. You will need to top up the water from time to time.

When the beans are cooked, remove the vegetables, herbs and red chilli. Chop up the chilli and discard the rest. Add the smoked paprika and chopped chilli to the beans. Stir through the piquillo pepper, rocket, lemon juice and a drizzle of olive oil.

For the sea bass, preheat a frying pan until hot and add a little olive oil. Season the bass skin and fry the fillets skin-side down until crisp. Turn the fillets over, add the butter and a squeeze of lemon and cook for a further minute.

To serve, place a spoonful of the beans on a plate and top it with the bass. Squeeze over the remaining lemon juice and drizzle with olive oil.

shoulder of lamb cooked in hay and lavender

It is a bit of an effort finding fresh hay and lavender that haven't been treated with pesticides and are suitable for cooking, but if you can, this dish is a real crowd pleaser.

serves 4

1 large shoulder good-quality lamb, bone in
250g unsalted butter, softened
salt and pepper
a few sprigs of fresh rosemary and thyme
enough fresh hay to fill your pot
1 small bunch of freshly cut lavender, around 50g or so
1 garlic bulb, smashed up into cloves, skin and all
1 large twig of bay leaves
150ml white wine

Preheat the oven to 180°C/350°F/gas mark 4. Smear the lamb with the softened butter and season. In a heavy cooking pot (preferably one with a lid) put a layer of all the fresh herbs, half the hay and all the lavender at the bottom. Add the garlic and bay leaves.

Lay the buttered lamb in the pot and pack in the rest of the hay. Add the white wine, pop on the lid and roast in the preheated hot oven for 1½–2 hours, depending on the size of the shoulder and the desired pinkness of the meat. Initially leave the pot untouched for at least 1½ hours. Check the meat with a skewer. Leave it inserted for 20 seconds: if it comes out warm/hot the meat should be medium rare; if it burns your top lip then it's almost certainly well done. Remove from the hay and carve normally. Serve with vegetables of your choice.

sweet and sour shallots

You can keep these in the fridge for a few weeks but they'll probably get eaten quickly.

fills 1 x 450g jar

20–25 round shallots, peeled
olive oil
2 tbsp light brown sugar
2 tbsp balsamic vinegar
2 tbsp red wine vinegar
fresh thyme sprigs
salt and pepper

Colour the shallots in a large frying pan in a little olive oil. Stir in the sugar and cook to brown and caramelize. Add the vinegars to deglaze the pan, stirring. Boil to reduce with the thyme sprigs, then season to taste. Cool and serve or store in the fridge.

roast chicken with bay leaves and preserved lemon

This is a great one-pot dish, which should take little over an hour to cook and elevates the humble chicken to new heights! The preserved lemon can be picked up at most good supermarkets now so don't substitute it with a regular lemon. The saltiness the preserved ones bring is integral to this dish.

serves 4–6

1 large free-range chicken, rinsed (approx. 1.5kg)
1 whole preserved lemon
1 bunch of fresh basil
1 twig of bay leaves
salt and pepper
extra virgin olive oil
2 garlic bulbs, cut in half
2 slices of grilled bruschetta per person

Preheat the oven to 200°C/400°F/gas mark 6.

Simply stuff the chicken with the whole preserved lemon, the basil and bay leaves. Season inside and out, rub with olive oil and put in a roasting tin.

Roast in the preheated oven with the garlic scattered around the bird for at least an hour, basting regularly. Check after an hour and allow longer depending on the size of the bird, but generally no longer than another 20 minutes. To check if the chicken is cooked, insert a skewer into the flesh – if the juices that run out are transparent, it is done, and if the juices are pink, the bird needs longer.

When the chicken is cooked allow to rest somewhere warm and catch any resting juices. Leave for at least 15 minutes.

When ready to serve, remove the lemon from the cavity and smear the roasted garlic on to the grilled toasts (it should be rather molten). Chop up some of the preserved lemon and scatter over the garlic toast. Flash through the oven to warm while slicing the chicken.

Serve the chicken over the garlic toast with the juices from the roasting tin.

sardines and caramelized onion tart

This dish is great fun to make and looks really dramatic. It doesn't usually manage to reach the table, the children and I like to eat big chunks with our fingers.

serves 4
500g bought or homemade puff pastry
4 large onions, peeled, halved and finely sliced
50ml olive oil
a few sprigs of fresh thyme, leaves picked
salt and pepper
1 large tbsp olives, stoned and roughly chopped
10 fresh sardine fillets, pin-boned, heads removed but tails intact

On a floured surface, roll out the puff pastry to a 30cm circle, transfer to a floured baking sheet, then fold over the edges and press with your fingers to make a rustic-looking crimped edge, about 3mm thick. Prick with a fork all over and put in the fridge to chill.

In a frying pan, caramelize the onion slowly in the olive oil – this will take about 1–1½ hours. Add the thyme and then salt and pepper at the end to season. Reserve.

Preheat the oven to 200°C/400°F/gas mark 6.

Cook the puff pastry base in the preheated oven for 15 minutes or so until golden brown.

Remove from the oven and spread over the onions and a few thyme sprigs, leaving a border of pastry all round, avoiding the crimped edge. Sprinkle over the olives and lay the fillets of sardines all round in a circle like the spokes of a wheel. Bake for 20 minutes or so until the sardines are cooked through.

Cut into thick wedges to serve.

tomatoes and mozzarella on brioche

This is my favourite snack. Proper fast food, it takes 10 minutes start to finish and is totally delicious, just as long as the tomatoes are good quality and ripe and the mozzarella is super fresh.

serves 2

25g salted butter
salt and pepper
4 plum or 2 beef tomatoes, the ripest and most flavoursome,
  sliced lengthways
4 anchovy fillets
120g crème fraîche
2 balls buffalo mozzarella, torn into pieces
a few basil leaves
2 slices of large brioche loaf

Heat the butter in a frying pan until foaming, then season the tomatoes and sauté, cut-side down, for 5 minutes or so. Turn the tomatoes over and cook for a further 5 minutes. Add the anchovy fillets and mash to dissolve.

Stir in the crème fraiche, then bring to the boil to thicken. Throw in the mozzarella, then add the basil. Stir two or three times and remove from the heat.

Toast the slices of brioche and spoon the tomatoes over them. Serve.

red wine poached strawberries with cinnamon toast

Ideally use a light, summer-drinking red, like a Fleurie or Pinot Noir, to make the most of this dish.

serves 4

900g strawberries
400ml light red wine
100–130g caster sugar, to taste
1 vanilla pod, split lengthways
1 cinnamon stick

Cinnamon toast
250g bought or homemade puff pastry
1 large egg, beaten
1 tsp ground cinnamon
1 pinch of sea salt

Wipe and hull the strawberries. Bring the wine, sugar, vanilla and cinnamon to a gentle boil in a saucepan. Drop the strawberries into the red wine. Bring to the boil and immediately remove from the heat and cover. Set aside until the wine and strawberries have cooled. At this stage the fruit should be perfectly poached, soft yet still holding its shape.

Preheat the oven to 200°C/400°F/gas mark 6.

For the cinnamon toast, roll out the pastry on a floured surface into two rectangles about 5mm thick and chill in the fridge on a baking sheet. Remove and brush one rectangle with beaten egg and scatter over the cinnamon. Sprinkle lightly with sea salt. Cover with the second layer of pastry and push together. Prick all over with a fork, brush with more egg and chill for another 20 minutes.

Bake in the preheated oven for 10–15 minutes until golden. Remove and cool. Cut into 1cm fingers and serve warm with the poached strawberries.

pain perdu with damsons and clotted cream

Poached damsons yield the most beautiful colour when cooked and their tartness sits well with the sweetness of the fried toast. The cooking liquor left over makes the most delicious sorbet.

serves 4

1kg fresh damsons, cut in half and stoned
250ml rich fruity red wine
finely grated zest and juice of 1 orange
1 cinnamon stick
150g caster sugar
clotted cream, to serve

Pain perdu
1 brioche loaf or fruity panettone, sliced about 1cm thick
3 medium eggs, beaten
1 pinch of ground allspice or mixed spice
50g salted butter

In a saucepan, bring the wine, orange zest and juice, the cinnamon stick and about 125g sugar to the boil. Remove and pour over the damsons. If the damsons are ripe, simply cover and leave to soften; if they are still a bit hard, cook gently in the juices for 5–10 minutes. Taste and add more sugar if necessary.

For the pain perdu, dip the bread into the beaten eggs, and sprinkle with some sugar and a pinch of the allspice on both sides. Pan-fry in gently foaming butter until golden brown on both sides.

Serve the damsons spooned over the pain perdu with a spoonful of clotted cream.

teisen lap with lavender honey and roasted figs

The Welsh cake, teisen lap, is a very traditional spiced, moist fruit cake. Use the best figs you can find, from Provence, Italy or Greece. Leave the Brazilian ones well alone! For the lavender honey, simply infuse a good-quality honey with a small bunch (3–4 sprigs) of dried lavender to taste. Leave to mature in the jar, then use as you would plain honey.

serves 4–6

Teisen lap
300g sultanas
300ml strong tea (Earl Grey is good)
385g unsalted butter
385g caster sugar
6 medium eggs
385g self-raising flour
3 generous tsp mixed spice
finely grated zest of 1 orange and 1 lemon

Roast figs
12 fresh figs, ripe black or green ones
50g unsalted butter, melted
300–400ml good-quality lavender honey

clotted cream and 8–10 sprigs of dried lavender, to serve

Preheat the oven to 180°C/350°F/gas mark 4. Grease and line a 25 x 35cm baking tin.

Pre-soak the sultanas in the freshly brewed tea and set aside.

Cream the butter and sugar together in a bowl until white and fluffy. Whisk the eggs. Slowly add the egg to the creamed butter and sugar, adding 1 tbsp of the flour to prevent splitting.

Fold the flour and mixed spice into the creamed mix and finally fold in the drained sultanas, lemon and orange zest. Transfer into the prepared baking tin and bake in the preheated oven for about 1 hour or until a sharp knife inserted into the middle comes out clean. Remove from the oven and turn the temperature up to 200°C/400°F/gas mark 6.

Meanwhile, to roast the figs, put in an ovenproof dish and simply cut across from the tip of the fig downwards three-quarters of the way and pinch open. Dot with some melted butter and drizzle with some of the lavender honey. Roast in the high oven with a splash of water for 10 minutes or until the figs are just about to collapse.

Serve the teisen lap warm, sliced into squares, with a couple of whole roasted figs on top. Drizzle with some more lavender honey and a dollop of clotted cream. Decorate with sprigs of dried lavender.

summer fruit gratin

Don't be put off by the 'gratin' element. This dish is simple, delicious and quite startlingly beautiful. You will have some meringue and custard left over because it is difficult to make them in smaller quantities. But the custard, for instance, will keep well in the fridge for a few days, so can be used for another dish.

serves 4–6

500ml milk
1 vanilla pod, split lengthways
6 medium egg yolks
150g caster sugar
75g plain flour
8 medium egg whites
lemon juice
1 splash of rum, brandy or eau de vie
400–500g summer fruit (nectarines, strawberries, raspberries,
peaches, redcurrants, or any other fruits and berries you prefer)

Put the milk in a saucepan with the vanilla pod, heat through gently and set aside to infuse.

Whisk the egg yolks and half the sugar together in a bowl until pale. Tip in the flour and stir to make a paste, then whisk in the warm, strained milk.

Return the mix to the stove, and stir until thickened and there's no trace of flour. Set aside.

Preheat the grill.

Put the egg whites in a large clean bowl, add a squeeze of lemon juice and beat them until they treble in size, adding a little of the remaining sugar (they should hold their own weight and look like a glossy meringue).

Take a large spoon of the reserved custard mix and throw in a dash of booze, and then fold in most of the meringue.

Scatter the soft fruits on to a plate and spoon over the gratin mix. Place under a scorching hot grill, or attack with a blowtorch, until the gratin has turned golden brown on the peaks and the mixture does not move about when gently shaken. Serve immediately.

hazelnut shortbreads

The hazelnuts can be substituted with other nuts, and a handful of raisins thrown into the mix is also good. These biscuits are easy and quick to make, and sturdy enough to keep in an airtight container for a few days.

makes as many or few as you like, depending on size

300g shelled hazelnuts
300g unsalted butter
25g light brown sugar
350g plain flour
1 pinch of ground allspice
icing sugar, to dust

Preheat the oven to 180°C/350°F/gas mark 4, and grease a large baking sheet.

Toast the hazelnuts in a dry frying pan until golden and then blitz in a food processor.

Blend the butter and sugar together in a bowl, then mix in the flour, allspice and the blitzed hazelnuts.

Shape however desired on the prepared baking sheet. I make these into quenelles using 2 dessertspoons, but they will taste just as good shaped into small rounds. Cook in the preheated oven for 10–15 minutes until golden brown.

Remove, cool on a wire rack and dust with icing sugar.

SEPTEMBER • OCTOBER

SEPTEMBER AND OCTOBER

Just as I become bored with the barbecue and the weather begins to change, so does the food on offer. But that's the beauty of eating with the seasons. Sweetcorn is usually the first sign to me that summer is on the way out, and just as this happens the first girolle mushrooms appear, so these two old friends always end up on my menus in a dish together.

The lightness of summer tends to edge out gradually with the appearance of apples, pears, pumpkins and squashes. These to my mind are the forerunners of the big winter veg to come. I have become a big fan of quince since moving to Wales and gaining access to the local supply. We use them in various ways, particularly to create a more aromatic crumble than with just apples or pears, and as quince paste to serve with our local cheeses.

Another exciting ingredient that signals the end of summer is the whimberry. These are small berries with a delicious, subtle flavour, which grow up on the Black Mountains. They are like bilberries and other similar regional fruit, and although difficult to harvest, being so small, are well worth the trouble. Apart from puddings, I like to serve them with red meat dishes in the same way I'd use the similarly abundant elderberry.

As the temperature drops and cool, crisp mornings become the norm, we are prompted to crave bigger and more robust dishes. So my advice is to indulge in the lighter, more vibrant textures and flavours before the comfort food season kicks in.

black pudding, smoked eel, caramelized apples and cider mustard sauce

This recipe throws together such a great combination of seasonal ingredients to make a simple and delicious autumnal dish. It does make a difference if you can source some good-quality black pudding: your butcher should be able to help you out here. This is the kind of earthy, country food that I adore.

serves 4

4 thick slices of best-quality black pudding
olive oil
400g smoked eel fillets, cut into long angled pieces
watercress or parsley, to garnish

Cider mustard sauce
150g unsalted butter
1 white onion, peeled and finely diced
1 garlic clove, peeled and crushed
2 sprigs fresh of thyme
100ml cider vinegar
330ml dry cider

250ml chicken stock (*see* page 296)
200ml double cream
1 tbsp Dijon mustard
1 tbsp wholegrain mustard
salt and pepper

Caramelized apples
3 Cox's apples, unpeeled but cored and quartered (rub with lemon juice to stop oxidation)
100g unsalted butter
150g soft brown sugar
100ml cider vinegar

To make the cider mustard sauce, in a saucepan, melt the butter and sweat off the onion with the garlic clove and the thyme. When translucent add the cider vinegar and cider, and reduce until almost gone. Add the chicken stock and reduce by half. Add the cream and bring to the boil. Add the mustards now. Taste and season. Reserve.

To caramelize the apples, sauté them in a warm frying pan in the butter and allow to turn golden brown. Add the brown sugar and cider vinegar, and cook until the apples are soft and golden in colour. Remove from the heat and reserve.

Fry the black pudding in some olive oil until crisp on the outside and hot in the middle. This should take about 3–4 minutes.

Arrange the black pudding on 4 plates. Spoon the caramelized apples over the top. Place 4–5 pieces of eel over the top of each and spoon round the cider mustard sauce. Garnish with some watercress or parsley.

elderberry, pigeon and snail bruschetta

I get very overexcited about this kind of earthy, gutsy food. It's simply the best the season has to offer, put together in a sympathetic way.

serves 2

1 wood pigeon or farmed squab, rinsed
salt and pepper
1 splash of ruby port
1 heaped tbsp fresh elderberries
50g butter
1 sprig of fresh thyme
1 garlic clove, peeled and crushed
1 shallot, peeled and diced
6 snails, pre-prepared (fresh, canned or frozen)
a few shelled cobnuts (or hazelnuts)
1 small handful of flat-leaf parsley leaves, roughly chopped

Bruschetta
2 slices stale country-style bread or ciabatta
1 garlic clove, peeled
extra virgin olive oil

Preheat the grill or char-grill, and preheat the oven to 180°C/350°F/gas mark 4.

Spatchcock the bird by removing the backbone and flattening it out (your butcher should do this for you). Season and char-grill for 3–4 minutes on both sides to colour and start the cooking. Put into a roasting tin and roast in the preheated oven for a further 4–5 minutes for rare, depending upon the thickness of the bird. When done, there should be a slight spring in the breast, and the flesh should be pink all the way through but not flabby. Remove the tin from the oven, and throw in a slug of port and the elderberries. Allow the bird to rest in the tin to collect any juices; this will be the finished sauce.

In a frying pan, heat half the butter, the thyme, garlic and shallot together. When it starts to foam, chuck in the snails and sauté off for a few minutes. Add the cobnuts and toast for a further few minutes to colour. Add the parsley. Remove and reserve.

Finally, char-grill the bread on both sides, rub with a raw garlic clove and lightly sprinkle with good olive oil. Quarter the pigeon, allowing half per person, and place on the bread. Scatter over the snails and cobnuts, and lightly dress with the cooking juices, port and elderberries. Serve.

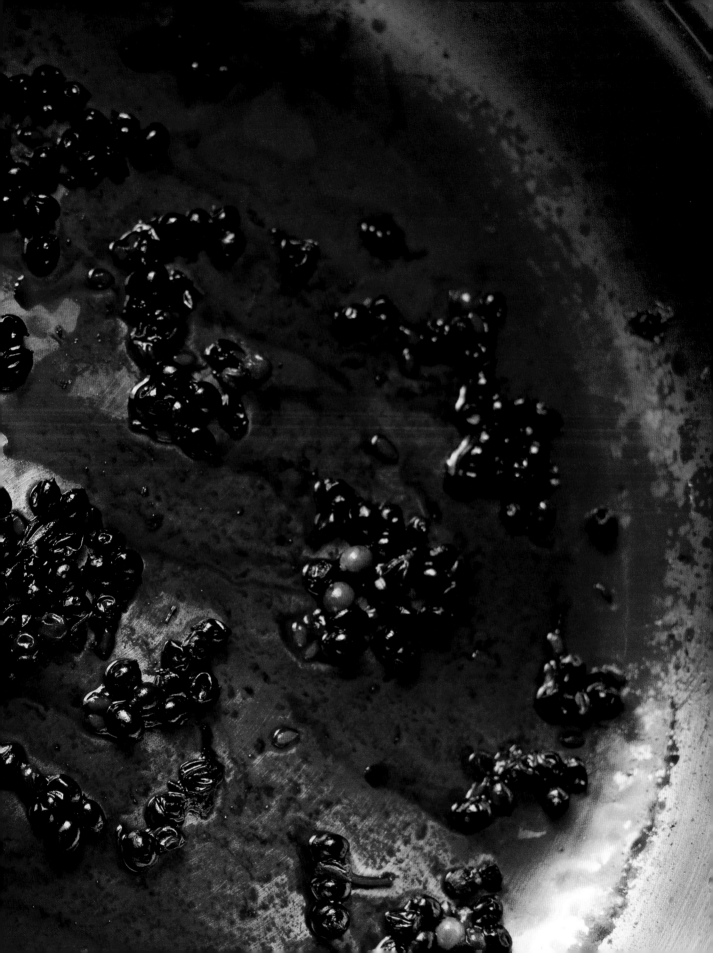

loin of hogget, walnuts and rock samphire

This is a very quick yet impressive starter dish, using great ingredients and no-fuss cooking. Hogget is nothing more than a mature lamb between the ages of one and two years. The fat is much sweeter than that of lamb and the flesh is darker and richer in appearance and taste. To my mind, hogget is the superior choice for those in the know!

serves 4 as a starter

1 x 8-bone loin of hogget

1 tsp black peppercorns

2 garlic cloves, peeled

2 fresh rosemary sprigs, leaves picked

2–3 tbsp extra virgin olive oil

50g butter

1 handful of freshly cracked walnuts

salt and pepper

150g rock samphire

1 splash of walnut oil (optional)

Preheat the oven to 200°C/400°F/gas mark 6.

Seal off the loin of hogget in a hot frying pan. Crush the peppercorns, garlic and rosemary in a pestle and mortar, rub on the meat and roast in the oven for 15 minutes or so in the olive oil, depending on your favoured degree of cooking for lamb. This dish is best served medium rare – the hogget should be pink in the middle. Once cooked, remove the rack of hogget from the oven and reserve all the important meat juices.

In another frying pan heat the butter until nut brown in colour, add the walnuts and season lightly. Shake the nuts about to extract the flavour, and then add the samphire to wilt. This will take 2–3 minutes.

While this is going on, slice the hogget from the bone, cut into thinnish slices, allowing 3–4 slices per person. To assemble the dish simply spoon the samphire and walnuts on to 4 plates, lay the pieces of meat about and spoon over the meat juices mixed with a good-quality walnut oil, if desired. Serve.

langoustines with pumpkin and ginger purée

This can be served in individual portions or, if you think there won't be a fight, serve on a big platter for digging in and sharing.

serves 4 as a starter

100g fresh pumpkin seeds

salt and pepper

24 medium or 16 large langoustines

olive oil

lemon juice

Pumpkin and ginger purée

1 small pumpkin, about 1.5–2kg in weight, peeled and diced

80–100g fresh root ginger, peeled and sliced

1 tbsp coriander seeds

75g unsalted butter

100ml double cream

Toast off the pumpkin seeds in a dry pan and when lightly toasted, toss in some salt and pepper to taste. Leave to one side.

In a saucepan, sweat the diced pumpkin, ginger and coriander seeds off in two-thirds of the butter for 10–20 minutes, without colouring. Cover barely with water (or stock) and simmer until tender, some 20–30 minutes. Just before ready to remove from the heat, add the cream and bring to the boil. With a slotted spoon, remove the pumpkin and place in a blender. Purée with the remaining butter. Push through a sieve, if so desired, for a smoother result.

Preheat the oven to 200°C/400°F/gas mark 6.

Lay the langoustines in a roasting tray and liberally splash over some good olive oil, some salt and pepper and lemon juice. Roast for 10–15 minutes until the shells start to lighten and slightly char. Baste them in the olive oil and lemon juice throughout the cooking.

To serve, pile the langoustines up on 4 plates, with the pumpkin purée on the side and toasted pumpkin seeds scattered over. Simply peel off the shells and dip the tails into the purée.

grilled squid, merguez sausage and couscous

This dish has got North African overtones. The spicy merguez sausage contains oils that, when cooked, mix beautifully with the squid and couscous.

serves 2

50ml extra virgin olive oil

2 merguez sausages

250g fresh squid, cleaned, the bodies opened flat
 (score these for a more decorative result)

sea salt and pepper

1 pinch of hot smoked paprika

Couscous

about 150g couscous

finely grated zest of 1 lemon

½ bunch fresh coriander, chopped

1 handful of flat-leaf parsley leaves, chopped

1 fine fresh red chilli, chopped

1 banana shallot, peeled and finely sliced

100ml red wine vinegar

a few tbsp of caster sugar

Preheat the oven to 180°C/350°F/gas mark 4, and preheat the grill or char-grill.

First the couscous. Put the dried stuff in a bowl and barely cover with boiling water. Cover and leave somewhere warm for 10 minutes. Fork through the couscous and add some salt and pepper, the lemon zest, fresh herbs, chilli and shallot. In a small pan heat the red wine vinegar and sugar together until sweet and sour. Add this to the couscous as well, and stir through.

Put half the oil in a small roasting tin, add the sausages and cook for 5 minutes or so in the preheated oven. Let rest to collect some of the oils that come off.

Char-grill the squid with a sprinkling of sea salt until it starts to lift off the grill. Remove, drizzle over the remaining oil and leave to rest with the sausages.

To assemble, slice the sausage and jumble with the squid. On each plate, pile up the couscous, top with the squid and sausage, drizzle with some of the cooking oils from the sausage and throw a pinch of smoked paprika at the dish. Finished.

stewed octopus, smoked paprika, tomato and basil

This is one of my favourite seafood dishes. Octopus is not daunting in any way once you know how. Either cook it very quickly or very slowly. Both produce tender results. Anything in between will be tough as old boots. Freezing the octopus also helps to tenderize it.

serves 4

1 large frozen octopus, defrosted and cleaned
4 ripe tomatoes, crushed a bit by hand
1 bunch of fresh basil, leaves picked, stalks retained
  (and tied together)
1 garlic bulb, cut in half
1 generous pinch of flaked sea salt
1 fresh red chilli
2 bay leaves
2 tsp smoked paprika
200ml extra virgin olive oil

Preheat the oven to 150°C/300°F/gas mark 2.

Throw the whole octopus, tomatoes, basil stalks, cut garlic, salt, chilli, bay leaves and smoked paprika into a solid braising pot with a good-fitting lid. Pour over the olive oil.

Put the pot into the oven and check after 1½ hours. The octopus should be tender. Check by attempting to cut its tentacle with a spoon. If this proves difficult, put it back in the oven for another 20 minutes. Keep checking in this way until tender. Remove and allow to cool in the pot. The flavour of this dish improves with resting.

To serve, cut some of the octopus into chunks, reheat in its juices and throw in the basil leaves. This dish is particularly good with some potatoes, cooked in the octopus liquor, or suitable fresh pasta, such as penne.

scallops and razor clams

It upsets me to walk along a beach, crunching razor-clam shells underfoot and then not being able to find a seaside restaurant that serves them. If you are digging for the clams yourself, it can be great fun but a bit tricky. Find their blow-holes in the sand and pour some salt water in: it should make them rise to the surface.

serves 4

2 garlic cloves, peeled and finely sliced
best-quality extra virgin olive oil
8 slices of good-quality cured ham (Parma, Coppa or Iberico), chopped into slivers
12 razor clams, in shell
175ml oloroso sherry
½ tsp smoked paprika
2 tbsp finely chopped fresh flat-leaf parsley
8 king scallops, out of shell and cleaned
salt and pepper

Soak the razor clams in salted water for 1 hour, then rinse them well in cold, running water for 10 minutes to remove any sand, discarding any that don't close when handled.

Have 2 frying pans hot and ready to go. In the first pan, fry off the garlic slivers in some of the olive oil for a minute to extract the flavour but not too far, as they may blacken. If this happens, discard and start again. Throw in the ham and sauté for a further minute.

Now add the razor shells and the sherry. Allow to boil furiously to open the razor clams, discarding any that do not open. Once opened, stir in the smoked paprika and parsley. Keep warm.

In the other pan sear off the scallops in a little more of the oil for no more than 1 minute each side, until lightly golden in colour. Season. Throw the scallops and any juices into the razor clams, toss and serve. This is good served with the flatbread on page 212.

sweetcorn soup with girolles and tarragon

This soup is nearly always on my menu throughout September, both girolles and sweetcorn being great seasonal partners. Sautéed together, they make an excellent accompaniment to a very good piece of fish, such as turbot.

serves 4

2 onions, peeled and roughly chopped
½ head of celery, roughly chopped
50g unsalted butter
olive oil
3 sprigs of fresh tarragon, leaves and stalks separated
2 bay leaves
salt and pepper
8 whole sweetcorn cobs, stripped of the corn
1 garlic bulb, cut in half
water or chicken stock (*see* page 296)
50g girolles or other wild mushrooms per person

In a frying pan, fry off the onions and celery in the butter and 1tbsp or so of olive oil until soft. Add the tarragon stalks for flavour plus the bay leaves. Season.

Throw in the corn and garlic, barely cover with water or chicken stock and simmer for 20–40 minutes until the corn is well cooked. Purée the soup in a blender and push through a sieve. Reserve.

Fry off the mushrooms in a little olive oil, and season with salt and pepper. Chuck in the finely chopped tarragon leaves. Heat the soup through and serve garnished with the mushrooms.

sweet lemon, ginger and walnut pasta

I first tried this in a back-street restaurant in Florence. It was one of those jaw-dropping moments when you become transfixed by the dish in front of you. After much cajoling, the grandmother behind the stove scribbled something in Italian on a scrap of paper...

serves 2–4

1 lemon, peeled of the rind, no white pith
5 garlic cloves, peeled
1 tbsp thyme leaves
1 tsp ground mixed spice
5 tbsp runny honey
1 tbsp caster sugar
extra virgin olive oil
2 tbsp flat-leaf parsley leaves, roughly chopped
30g puréed fresh root ginger, sieved of stringy bits
15 fresh or dried shelled walnuts, plus extra to garnish
water or vegetable stock (*see* page 297)
salt and pepper
100g bucatini or spaghetti per person

Blitz three-quarters of the lemon rind with all the ingredients up to the walnuts in a food processor. Let down the mixture with a ladleful of hot water or vegetable stock, just to loosen. Now add the walnuts and continue to purée. Season with salt and pepper.

Boil up some bucatini or spaghetti until al dente, drain then add 4–5 tbsp of the purée and toss. Add some more of the pasta boiling water if necessary to coat the pasta.

Sprinkle over some more chopped walnuts with the remaining chopped lemon zest and serve immediately.

calf's liver, borlotti beans and sherry vinaigrette

It's important to always use the best-quality liver you can. The acidity of the sherry vinegar is an essential element here, as it acts as a balance against the richness of the liver.

serves 2

2 pieces of calf's liver, about 1cm thick and about 200g each in weight, rinsed
25g butter
salt and pepper

Beans
about 200g podded fresh borlotti beans
1 onion, peeled and cut in half
1 carrot, whole
1 celery stick
1 garlic bulb, cut in half
3 bay leaves
10g fresh thyme
smoked bacon scraps

Vinaigrette
200ml mixed sunflower oil and peanut oil
50ml sherry vinegar
½ tsp Dijon mustard
½ garlic clove, peeled and crushed
3 fresh sage leaves, roughly chopped

Firstly cook the borlotti beans. Put the beans, onion, carrot, celery, aromatics and bacon scraps in a saucepan. Cover with cold water and simmer for 30–40 minutes until tender. Do not season until the end of the cooking.

Make the vinaigrette by mixing all the ingredients, except the sage, together in a bowl to emulsify before adding the fresh chopped sage.

To cook the liver, gently heat the butter until foaming. Season the liver and pan-fry for 2 minutes until the liver starts to colour. Turn over and cook for another minute. Remove and keep warm.

To finish the dish, dress the beans with the vinaigrette. Place the liver on top and serve.

rump of welsh lamb, spiced aubergine, mint yoghurt and flatbread

This dish is based on the now classic imam bayeldi, which is delicious on its own, but works equally well with lamb.

serves 4

4 lamb rumps or chumps
a few sprigs of fresh rosemary
6 garlic cloves
1 knob of butter
3 aubergines, cut into chunks
olive oil
salt and pepper
2 onions, peeled and diced
1 tsp ground allspice
½ tsp ground cumin
1 pinch of cayenne pepper

100g currants
1 x 500g can plum tomatoes
4–5 fresh plum tomatoes, roughly chopped
½ bunch each of fresh coriander and
  mint, chopped, plus extra to garnish

Mint yoghurt
1 garlic clove, peeled
a few sprigs of fresh mint
white pepper
4 tbsp Greek yoghurt

Preheat the oven to 200°C/400°F/gas mark 6.

In a roasting tin, roast the lamb in a hot oven until pink, about 10–12 minutes. When out of the oven and resting, throw the rosemary sprigs, 2 garlic cloves and a knob of butter into the tin, and baste from time to time.

Dice the aubergine into 1cm cubes and fry in a frying pan in some olive oil until golden brown all over and soft. Season lightly with salt. Set aside.

In a saucepan, sweat off the diced onion in some olive oil with the remaining whole garlic cloves. When translucent, after 10 minutes or so, add the spices and fry them off for 1 minute. Throw in the currants and canned tomatoes and cook for a further couple of minutes. Stir in the fresh tomatoes, followed by the aubergine chunks. Check the seasoning and add the freshly chopped herbs. Set aside.

Make the mint yoghurt by crushing the garlic clove with a few sprigs of fresh mint along with a little salt and white pepper in a pestle and mortar. Stir this into the yoghurt and allow the flavours to mingle in the fridge.

Cut the lamb into thickish slices. Arrange next to a pile of aubergine and spoon the yoghurt dressing over. Garnish with mint leaves and serve with warm flatbread (*see* page 212).

grilled flatbread

This will make more than enough, but the dough is pretty good turned into a focaccia bread or even a quick pizza base. It keeps very well in the fridge for a few days.

serves 4–6

15g fresh yeast
2–3 tbsp lukewarm water
500g strong bread flour
½ tsp salt
1 tbsp olive oil, plus extra for drizzling
10 tbsp water, and extra if needed
1 sprinkle of sea salt, to serve

Crumble the yeast into a bowl, then whisk in the lukewarm water. Sift the flour and salt into a separate bowl. Make a well in the middle. Pour the yeast water into the well in the flour and add the olive oil and 10 tbsp water. Mix to form a dough. Add another tbsp or more of water, if necessary, to make it nice and workable. Knead the dough on a floured surface until it is soft and pliable, about 10 minutes.

Place the dough in a bowl, cover loosely and leave to prove in a warm place for a few hours. Remove the dough from the bowl and knead lightly, for about 5 minutes, to knock back. Cover and leave in the fridge. When required, rip a small amount of dough off and roll out into disc shapes, roughly the size of a small saucer, allowing 1 per person. Char-grill or throw on to a very hot, dry frying pan for 1–2 minutes each side until charred and cooked through. Drizzle with olive oil and sprinkle with sea salt to serve.

cobnut and parsley relish

This seasonal relish is particularly good with simple grilled lamb chops or roast chicken. It's also good with freshly grilled sardines. If you can't get hold of cobnuts, do something else instead, it's not really worth substituting in this case.

serves 4

finely grated zest and juice of 1 lemon
2 shallots, peeled and finely diced
10g fresh mint leaves, roughly chopped
50g fresh flat-leaf parsley leaves, roughly chopped
4 tbsp freshly cracked cobnuts, roasted and chopped
100–150ml hazelnut oil

Mix the first five ingredients together in a bowl and stir in the oil to bind to a loose paste.

roast grouse with sautéed salsify, endive and wet walnuts

Wet walnuts are simply the new season's crop. They have none of the bitterness associated with regular walnuts. In the restaurant we can get them foraged locally; alternatively, a friendly grocer will be able to order them for you.

serves 2

1 grouse, rinsed
salt and pepper
olive oil
2 garlic cloves, peeled and crushed
1 sprig of fresh thyme
125ml Madeira
butter
2–3 pieces salsify, peeled and blanched until tender
2 Belgian endives (chicory)
1 squeeze of lemon juice
1 pinch of caster sugar
2 tbsp chopped wet walnuts

Remove the breasts from the grouse. Season them and pan-fry in a little olive oil over a medium heat with half the garlic and thyme. Turn over to cook both sides. When medium rare, after about 4–5 minutes (there should be a slight spring in the pinkish flesh when it is prodded), add the Madeira and a small knob of butter and allow to rest. You could use the rest of the grouse in a stock or pasta sauce.

Throw the prepared salsify into a hot frying pan with some butter and colour gently. Add the endive leaves, remaining thyme and garlic, some salt and pepper, the lemon juice and sugar.

Finally add the roughly chopped wet walnuts just to warm through. Serve with the sliced grouse breast.

roast partridge with fig, celery leaf and gorgonzola

I like to pair game birds with fruit. It tends to lighten the load. Partridge can be quite a delicate bird and could therefore be a good introduction to game for the novice game-eater.

serves 4

4 partridge, rinsed
4 bay leaves
4 sprigs of fresh rosemary
8–12 garlic cloves, peeled
salt and pepper
150g butter
8–12 rashers of streaky bacon
1 splash of red port

Salad
1 head of celery, leaves removed,
   tender inner stalks reserved

20g Gorgonzola cheese, at room
   temperature
4 large black figs
4–5 freshly cracked, wet walnuts
1 tbsp olive oil
1 tsp thyme leaves
1 garlic clove, peeled and crushed

Vinaigrette
200ml olive oil
50ml sherry vinegar or red wine vinegar

Preheat the oven to 200°C/400°F/gas mark 4.

Stuff the birds with the herbs and garlic, and season. Seal off in a frying pan of foaming butter to colour the birds all over. Cover the breasts with the bacon and roast in the preheated oven in a roasting tin for 10–15 minutes until pink. Remove from the oven. Throw the port into the tin and allow to rest for 10 minutes.

Meanwhile, make the salad. Pick the young yellowish celery leaves from the inside and chop the tenderest of the stalks at an angle. Roughly chop the leaves. Crumble the cheese and quarter the figs. Toast the walnuts in the olive oil, with some salt and pepper, the thyme and garlic. Allow to cool and then roughly chop. Make the vinaigrette by simply mixing the ingredients together in a bowl to emulsify.

To assemble the salad, toss the celery with the walnuts and dress with the vinaigrette. Scatter over the crumbled cheese and quartered figs.

Serve the birds all together on a large plate with a few finger bowls scattered about with 4 individual salads. Any remaining vinaigrette can be mixed with the cooking juices, then lightly drizzled over the partridges.

chilli and tomato chutney

The chilli seeds make this chutney pretty hot, so remove them if you prefer something milder. Serve with a good strong Cheddar.

makes 1 litre   **1 large onion, peeled and finely chopped**
50ml olive oil
5 tsp finely grated garlic
3 tsp finely grated fresh root ginger
6 fresh red chillies, roasted, skinned and chopped
3 tsp yellow mustard seeds, toasted
1kg canned tomatoes, or equal weight in ripe
  fresh tomatoes, skinned
250g caster sugar dissolved in 250g white
  wine vinegar
salt

In a saucepan, fry the onion in the olive oil for 10 minutes to soften, then throw in the garlic and ginger and cook for a further 5 minutes.

Add the chopped chilli, seeds and flesh, and throw in the mustard seeds and tomatoes. Stew down for 20 minutes until most of the liquid has evaporated.

Add the sugar and vinegar solution, and bring back to the boil. Season with salt, remove from the heat and allow to cool. Store in the fridge.

baked apples with calvados custard

Cooking doesn't have to be flash and fancy. This is quite old-fashioned in its way, but there never seems any need to mess about with something so good. Chefs always do too much of that.

serves 4

200g caster sugar
50ml water
Calvados, to taste
4 large Cox's apples
1 small jar best-quality mincemeat

Custard
500ml milk
1 vanilla pod, split lengthways
6 medium egg yolks
120g caster sugar
Calvados, to taste

Preheat the oven to 180°C/350°F/gas mark 4.

Start by making a caramel. Put the sugar and water into a saucepan and bring to the boil. Continue to boil until nicely caramelized and a dark caramel colour. Stop the caramel by adding a drop of Calvados. Remove from the heat and allow to cool.

Core the apples and run a knife round the middle to allow for expansion. Stuff with the mincemeat. Baste in the caramel and bake in the preheated oven for 20–30 minutes.

Meanwhile, make the custard. Heat the milk and vanilla together in a saucepan to infuse. Whisk the egg yolks and sugar together in a bowl until pale, then pour the warm milk on to the yolks, stirring all the time. Put the custard back into the pan and on to the heat to thicken, about 5–6 minutes. Add Calvados to taste. Keep warm.

Serve the baked apples with the Calvados custard.

quince and walnut crumble

A quince can seem pretty unpalatable when picked, but it turns pink and becomes softer, sweeter and more aromatic when cooked. Because of their high pectin content, they are particularly suitable for making jams, pastes and preserves, but they also add interest to a whole host of simple seasonal puddings. Quince and walnuts make a great seasonal pairing.

serves 4

1 vanilla pod, split lengthways
pared zest of 1 orange
1 cinnamon stick
1 star anise
1 bay leaf
caster sugar to taste (200g plus)
1 half-bottle Muscat dessert wine
3 quince
single cream, to serve

Crumble topping
50g shelled walnuts
60g plain flour
50g caster sugar
40g quick-cook polenta
1 pinch of salt
75g unsalted butter, chilled
2 drops vanilla extract

For the crumble, toast the walnuts in a dry pan, then blitz to fine crumbs in a food processor.

In a mixer, blend the flour, sugar, walnuts, polenta and salt. Add the chilled butter, slowly bit by bit, along with the vanilla extract. Chill on a baking sheet for 30 minutes.

Preheat the oven to 160°C/325°F/gas mark 3.

Break the chilled crumble up a bit and bake in the preheated oven for 30–40 minutes or until golden. Cool, and when cool enough to handle, break into smaller pieces again.

For the quince, put the aromatics and sugar in a saucepan, pour over the dessert wine and bring to the boil. Remove from the heat and leave to infuse for 30 minutes.

Peel and core the quince and cut carefully into quarters. Lay the pieces of quince in a small roasting tin and pour over the contents of the pan. Roast for 60–80 minutes at the same temperature as above, until tender and turned pink.

Assemble the crumble in a shallow dish. Put the hot quince in the bottom and scatter the cooked crumble over it. Flash under a preheated grill or through the oven, just to reheat. Serve warm with single cream.

spiced apple tarte tatin
with clotted cream

This is my daughter's favourite pudding – a spiced-up version of the classic French dessert and one of the first things I learnt to cook. It takes a while to master and requires investment in a really good pan – but is well worth the effort. You'll never have any leftovers serving this dish!

serves 2–3

3 Cox's apples, peeled and halved
100g unsalted butter, softened
100g caster sugar
1 cinnamon stick
1 star anise
1 vanilla pod, split lengthways
1 twist of black pepper
1 pinch of freshly grated nutmeg
200g bought or homemade puff pastry
clotted cream, to serve

Peel and core the apples, then cut in half from top to bottom. Set aside.

Press the butter into the base of a 20cm diameter copper/heavy-based pan with the back of a wooden spoon until it melts to completely cover the base. Sprinkle over the caster sugar in an even layer. Place the cinnamon stick, star anise, vanilla, pepper and nutmeg in the pan then lay the halved apples on top, cut-side facing up.

On a floured surface, roll out the puff pastry to 3mm thick or so, then cut around a plate about 3cm larger than the cooking pan. Place in the pan, pushing the pastry down between the side of the pan and the apples to create the sides of the tart. Make sure the whole pan is tightly packed. Prick the top all over to allow the steam to escape when cooking, then chill for 30 minutes or so.

Preheat the oven to 220°C/425°F/gas mark 7.

To cook, put the pan over a moderate heat and shake the pan every few minutes to prevent the apples from burning. Look for a golden caramel colour to appear around the side of the pan, after about 6–8 minutes. (At this point, if the pastry starts to melt, you've rolled it too thin. Remove, cool and start again.)

Bake in the preheated oven for 20–25 minutes, until the pastry is firm and golden. If you are not serving the tatin immediately, you can leave it in the pan and reheat it later, or you can turn it out warm and serve with clotted cream.

custard and nutmeg tart
with caramelized bananas

Another British classic, and one I'm quite partial to...

serves 10

1 litre double cream

2 vanilla pods, split lengthways

10 medium eggs, beaten

250g caster sugar

1 x blind-baked 30cm pastry tart shell (*see* page 144)

Caramelized bananas

2 tbsp walnut oil

50g icing sugar

3 bananas, peeled and sliced

Preheat the oven to 110°C/225°F/gas mark ¼.

For the custard tart filling, bring the cream and vanilla to the boil in a saucepan to infuse. Put the beaten eggs and sugar in a bowl, and pour over the warm cream, stirring well. Push through a sieve into a bowl.

Pour into the blind-baked pastry case and cook in the preheated low oven for about 1 hour or just until it's about to set. Turn the oven off and allow to cool.

When ready to eat, in a frying pan warm the walnut oil. Add the icing sugar and throw in the slices of banana. Toss about for a few minutes and serve alongside the custard tart.

wild raspberry and whisky jelly

The amount of alcohol in this recipe makes it quite boozy and expensive, so keep it for a special occasion.

serves 4–6

11 gelatine leaves
500ml whisky
750g sugar syrup (*see* page 265)
about 400g wild raspberries
single cream, to serve

First soak the gelatine leaves in cold water. Warm up the whisky in a saucepan, add the sugar syrup and stir in the gelatine. Put aside to cool.

Line a litre jelly mould with some of the jelly mix and leave in the fridge to firm up. Take out of the fridge and sprinkle a generous amount of raspberries on top of the set jelly, then spoon some more of the liquid jelly over the raspberries and replace in the fridge to create another layer. The jelly can be gently reheated to liquefy, just so long as it is never boiled. This will destroy the setting quality of the gelatine.

When the jelly next comes out of the fridge the fruit should be held firm in the mould. Top up with the rest of the mix and leave to fully set, preferably overnight.

Turn out and serve with single cream and a few more scattered raspberries.

tarte à la crème with wild whimberries

Whimberries are quite time-consuming to pick in a sufficient quantity, but if you can find some, they really are the most delightful berry to use in cooking. Abergavenny market usually has some when they're in season. I've used them here to spice up a couple of classic recipes – tarte à la crème and traditional Welsh cakes.

serves 6

400g bought or homemade puff pastry
2 vanilla pods, split lengthways
1 litre condensed milk
20–50g caster sugar

Whimberry compote
300g wild whimberries or fresh Dorset blueberries
caster sugar, to taste

To make the compote, warm the whimberries or blueberries in a saucepan gently, with just enough sugar to sweeten slightly, probably about 1 tsp. The berries will release their juice and just about lose their shape. Pull off the heat and reserve.

Preheat the oven to 190°C/375°F/gas mark 5.

To make the tart base, roll out the puff pastry ultra-thin on a floured surface, and use to line a 25cm tart tin. Chill for 15 minutes, then blind-bake (lined with greaseproof and baking beans) for 20 minutes.

Mix the vanilla pods and seeds into the condensed milk and heat in a saucepan until reduced to a setting consistency, which will take about 8–10 minutes. It is important to keep stirring, otherwise the mix could catch on the bottom and turn bitter. Add a touch of sugar to taste.

Pour this into the blind-baked tart shell and glaze with a blowtorch (or under the grill). Serve cold with the fruit compote.

warm welsh cakes with whimberry compote

I'm only a recent convert to Welsh cakes, preferably warm off the griddle, but my wife grew up on them and persuaded me to give them a go. They work really well with fruit compote and here I've used the local whimberries picked off the Blorenge.

makes a lot of Welsh cakes!

125g unsalted butter

250g self-raising flour

75g caster sugar

100g raisins

1 pinch of ground allspice

1 pinch of ground cinnamon

1 medium egg, beaten

unsalted butter, clotted cream and whimberry compote (*see* page 226), to serve

Rub the butter and flour together in a bowl to make a breadcrumb-like texture, then add the sugar, raisins and spices. Bind the mix with the beaten egg. Roll out to about 1cm thickness and cut to shape with a 7cm pastry cutter.

Heat a flat frying pan over a moderate heat and dry-fry the cakes for about 3 minutes on each side, until golden brown.

Serve warm with plenty of melting butter and whimberry compote, and an unhealthy dollop of clotted cream.

blackberry and apple
suet pudding

I like to use suet puddings as a change from sponge puddings. You can experiment with different fruit, but blackberry and apple make a perfect seasonal pairing.

serves 6–8

250g self-raising flour
1 pinch of salt
120g shredded suet
milk
290g blackberry jam
2 Cox's or Bramley apples, grated
custard or clotted cream, to serve

Sauce
60g butter
60g light brown sugar
60ml glucose syrup
2 tbsp water
90g flaked almonds

Preheat the oven to 200°C/400°F/gas mark 6.

Sift the flour and salt into a bowl. Throw in the suet and add enough milk to allow the mix to come together to a sticky dough. You might need about 100ml.

On a floured surface, roll the dough out to a large rectangle about 1cm thick. Spread over the jam and grated apple. Roll up lengthways.

Put the roll on to a baking sheet, brush with milk and bake in the preheated oven for 35–40 minutes until cooked.

Then bring the sauce ingredients to the boil together in a saucepan. Spoon this mixture over the top of the pudding and put back in the preheated oven for another 10 minutes until golden. Serve with custard or clotted cream.

chocolate and pear tart

Don't be tempted to cut into the tart for a few hours as the filling will still be very molten. This is a very gooey chocolate tart, even when set.

serves 8–10

4 medium eggs
180g caster sugar
250g unsalted butter
380g good dark chocolate, broken into pieces
4 poached pears, cut in half lengthways
Poire Williams (eau de vie)
1 x blind-baked 30cm pastry tart shell (*see* page 144)
double cream and icing sugar, to serve

Preheat the oven to 140°C/275°F/gas mark 1.

Whisk the eggs and sugar together until they have tripled in volume. Meanwhile, melt the butter and chocolate together in a bowl over a pan of hot water.

Toss the poached pears in 4 tbsp of Poire Williams and leave them to steep for a few minutes. Lay the poached pears cut-side down around the base of the tart, fat end towards the outside.

Now carefully pour the chocolate and butter mix into the eggs and sugar. Stop whisking and gently pour the chocolate mix over the top of the pears. Immediately put into the oven and bake for 10–15 minutes until small cracks start to appear around the outside of the chocolate. Remove and cool.

Serve with a big dollop of cream flavoured with a little icing sugar and Poire Williams.

NOVEMBER • DECEMBER

NOVEMBER AND DECEMBER

The winter weather stimulates big appetites and demands bold flavours, so it's good news for chefs that the game season is in full flow. We have a constant supply of pheasant from the local estates, which we like to make good use of in our Christmas menus instead of the dreaded turkey. I am also particularly partial to whole roast woodcock, and despite the reaction it gets from many onlookers, I think it's best served in its traditional dramatic fashion, innards, beak and all.

Rich game dishes and sticky braised meats make a good excuse to enjoy those big red wines you've not been sure what to drink with all year. In fact, I like to explore the top shelf of the bar in December and I put lots of dishes on the menu that benefit from a big splash from a spirit or liqueur bottle. It seems entirely appropriate and festive!

Puddings should definitely be of the comforting variety and the depths of winter call for an extra degree of decadence. Even if you usually avoid such treats, it's the one time of year you can let yourself go and be extravagant. Everything should be served bigger and richer – whole cheeses, an enormous goose, proper puddings.

It's the perfect time to try foods you wouldn't perhaps consider throughout the rest of the year, such as the best oysters and diver-caught scallops.

stuffed goose neck with cranberry sauce

In the run-up to Christmas, it's always a good idea to pre-prepare a few tasty dishes that can be pulled out of the fridge to feed extra guests or particularly greedy relatives... This may seem rather a ghoulish recipe, but it is really just utilizing the often overlooked bits of the bird.

serves 4 as a starter

1 large goose neck, rinsed
sea salt
1 large can duck or goose fat, enough to submerge the stuffed neck of goose
cranberry sauce, to serve

Stuffing
400g belly pork, minced
200g foie gras
salt and pepper
25ml port
15ml brandy
25ml Madeira
1 pinch each of ground nutmeg, cloves and ginger
1 tsp fresh thyme leaves
1 garlic clove, peeled and crushed

Peel back the goose skin from the bone of the neck and cut away the bone. Sprinkle with a light seasoning of salt, cover and leave in the fridge overnight.

Meanwhile make the stuffing. Mix all the ingredients together and pan-fry a little of the mix before tasting to check the seasoning. Adjust if necessary. Cover and marinate in the fridge overnight.

The following day, give the goose neck a quick rinse to remove excess salt. Turn the right way round again and sew up one end (or pin with a cocktail stick) to prevent the filling from escaping. Stuff the neck with as much of the filling as possible, making sure you don't split the skin. Tie up and secure the open end.

Submerge your newly made sausage in a saucepan of warm duck fat and cook on a very low heat, so that the fat is barely blipping, for 2 or more hours. Or alternatively, put the pan, covered with foil, in a preheated oven at about 150°C/300°F/gas mark 2 for 1½–2 hours.

Once cooked, the goose sausage can be stored in the fridge submerged in its fat for many weeks. To eat, simply remove from the fat and serve warm or cold, sliced, with cranberry sauce.

chestnut and bacon soup

A great winter soup. Chestnuts have a lovely sweetness to them. It's quite a filling number, what with the bacon and Parmesan, so would be suitable as a supper dish in its own right.

serves 6–8

6–8 garlic cloves, peeled and crushed
1 large white onion, peeled and diced
2 carrots, diced
2 celery sticks, diced
50g butter
2 tsp olive oil
1 sprig of fresh rosemary
salt and pepper
150g smoked bacon or pancetta, diced
1 tbsp tomato purée
500g prepared blanched chestnuts, roughly chopped
1 bay leaf
chicken stock (see page 296) or water, to cover
extra virgin olive oil and freshly grated Parmesan, to serve

Sweat the garlic, onion, carrot and celery off in a saucepan in the butter and oil with the rosemary for 10 minutes. Season lightly at this point.

Add the diced pancetta and continue to cook for a further 10 minutes. Stir in the tomato purée and cook out for a further 2–3 minutes. Add the chopped chestnuts and allow to cook for a few minutes.

Finally add the bay leaf and chicken stock or water, and simmer for 20–30 minutes. Check the seasoning.

Purée the soup in a blender, then pass through a sieve. Serve with a good slug of good-quality olive oil and some freshly grated Parmesan.

overleaf *A day at the office for Graham Waddington and James Swift at Trealy Farm, where they produce some of the finest charcuterie I've ever tasted.*

scallops, chestnut purée and crisp sage

I like to serve this chestnut purée with some grilled toast or fried bread alongside a variety of game birds, but I have discovered that it also works perfectly with some beautiful fresh scallops.

serves 4

12 fat scallops
1 knob of butter
12 sage leaves

Chestnut purée
1 white onion, peeled and finely chopped
50g salted butter
1 bay leaf
3 garlic cloves, peeled and sliced
2–3 sprigs of fresh thyme
1 star anise
500g pre-poached chestnuts
100ml double cream
salt and pepper

For the purée, sweat the onion off in a saucepan in half the butter with the bay leaf, garlic, thyme and star anise, about 10 minutes. When translucent, add the chestnuts and stir around to break up. Add enough water to cover the chestnuts and simmer for 20 minutes.

Pour in the double cream, bring to the boil and remove the anise and bay leaf. Purée in a blender with the remaining butter until very smooth. Check the consistency and if it's too thick add a little more water while the blender is still running. The consistency should be quite thick and should dollop off a spoon. Check the seasoning.

To cook the scallops, simply sauté off in a frying pan of foaming butter for 2–3 minutes. Throw in the sage to flavour at the last minute. Serve with the chestnut purée.

bloody mary oysters

The perfect hair of the dog, but I don't tend to wait for the morning after.

serves 2

6 rock oysters, opened and juices reserved
1 splash of sherry (fino)
1 pinch of celery salt

Bloody Mary mix
1 splash of Tabasco sauce
1 splash of Worcestershire sauce
1 splash of vodka
150ml tomato juice

Combine the Bloody Mary ingredients in a jug.

Lay an oyster into a shot glass. Cover with the Bloody Mary mix. Add a splash of sherry, some of the reserved oyster juice and a pinch of celery salt.

Then down in one!

oysters, vermouth and tarragon cream

The important thing here is not to overcook the oysters as they will become chewy.

serves 2 as a sizeable starter

1 shallot, peeled and finely diced
a few fresh tarragon sprigs, leaves and stalks separated
25g unsalted butter
1 shot of vermouth
100ml double cream
12 oysters
1 squeeze of lemon juice

In a saucepan, sweat the shallot and tarragon stalks in the butter for 5 minutes until soft.

Throw in the shot of vermouth, bring to the boil and reduce. Add the cream and bring to the boil, then simmer.

Now open the oysters, being careful to reserve the juices. Take the oysters from the shell.

In another pan, bring the oyster juices to the boil, drop the oysters in and remove from the heat. Cook for 30 seconds.

Tip some of the juices into the cream along with the chopped tarragon leaves. Spoon some of the cream mix into each shell. Place an oyster on each shell and a squeeze of lemon over each oyster. Serve immediately, while hot.

savoy cabbage and stilton soup

Some pre-poached chestnuts chopped into the soup before serving would be the perfect seasonal garnish.

serves 4

50g butter
1 white onion, peeled and diced
4 celery sticks, diced
1 tsp cumin seeds
3–4 garlic cloves, peeled and chopped
1 head Savoy cabbage, outer leaves and thick stalk discarded,
   finely shredded
1 bay leaf
a few sprigs of fresh thyme
salt and pepper
250ml water or chicken stock (*see* page 296)
1 bunch of fresh flat-leaf parsley, roughly chopped

Stilton cream
250g best-quality Stilton cheese
100ml double cream

Firstly beat the room temperature Stilton in a bowl until soft, then beat in the cream. Push through a sieve for a smoother finish. This can be tedious and is not entirely necessary – depending on what consistency you prefer. Set to one side.

In a hot saucepan, melt the butter, and sweat off the onion and celery with the cumin seeds and garlic. Add the Savoy cabbage and continue to sweat for 5–10 minutes or so. Add the bay and thyme, salt and pepper, and cover with the water or stock. Bring to the boil and simmer for 20 minutes.

At this stage, I quite like to serve the soup with all its roughness and textures but, should you desire, add a splash of cream and purée it to oblivion in a blender for a smoother end result. Season the finished soup with more salt and pepper if necessary.

Serve with a healthy dollop of the Stilton cream, just before serving. This will melt into the bowl, making a great combination with the cumin-scented soup. Stir in the parsley for a bit of colour.

goat's cheese flavoured with armagnac

This has its origins in the French countryside. It's a good fridge standby and becomes more potent with age.

serves 4

300g fresh goat's cheese
10g fresh thyme leaves
2 tbsp Armagnac
1 tbsp runny honey
salt and pepper

Mash all the ingredients together in a bowl and leave at room temperature for a few hours to mingle the flavours.

Serve before dessert with a few prunes soaked in Armagnac and some good-quality toasted nutty bread.

old spot cooked in milk, cinnamon, bay and lemon

This is a beautifully gentle way of cooking a loin of pork. The spices are reminiscent of those used extensively in South American cooking.

serves 4–6

1 whole loin best-quality Old Spot pork, about 3–4kg,
   boneless and skinless
salt and pepper
olive oil
2 white onions, peeled and cut into quarters
100g unsalted butter
3 garlic bulbs, cut in half
approx. 2 litres milk (enough to cover the pork)
pared zest and juice of 2 lemons
30g fresh coriander leaves
4–5 bay leaves
20g cinnamon sticks
10g mixed peppercorns
½ nutmeg, freshly grated
a few cloves

Preheat the oven to 150°C/300°F/gas mark 2.

Season the pork all over and seal in a little olive oil in a deep casserole big enough to hold the pork as a whole. Add the onions, butter and garlic, and let the pork sizzle to extract the flavour. Add the milk almost to cover, along with the lemon zest and half of the juice, the coriander, bay leaves and the spices.

Put into the low preheated oven and cook uncovered for 1½–2 hours until the bones pull away easily.

Remove the pork. Keep warm and skim the sauce of excess fat, taste and pour in the remaining lemon juice. Reduce to sauce consistency. The sauce should now be nicely curdled.

Cut the meat into slices and spoon over the sauce, soft onions and cinnamon sticks. Serve with some greens and herbed rice.

braised oxtail with seville orange

This oxtail is so tasty. It can be served with a very simple, traditional garnish like mash and greens, or you can layer the braised meat between sheets of lasagne for a slightly lighter dish.

serves 4

8 large oxtail chunks, bone in
1 bottle deep rich, red wine
a few black peppercorns
1 bay leaf
1 small bunch of fresh thyme
1 garlic bulb, cut in half
2 star anise
olive oil
seasoned plain flour
2 large white onions, peeled and diced
4 celery sticks, diced
4 carrots, diced
pared zest and juice of 2 Seville oranges
water, or beef or chicken stock (*see* page 296), to cover

Marinate the oxtail pieces overnight, covered in the fridge, in the red wine, with the peppercorns, herbs, garlic and star anise. The next day drain the oxtail and reserve the red wine and aromatics.

Preheat the oven to 140°C/275°F/gas mark 1.

Heat a film of oil in a large frying pan. Dust the oxtail in seasoned flour and fry off to seal the meat and colour on all sides. Remove from the pan. Throw in the diced veg and colour these off too. This should take 10–20 minutes. Put the oxtail and the aromatics back in the pan and add the reserved red wine. Cook until reduced by half.

Add the Seville orange juice and zest. Add some water or stock to cover the oxtail and cook in the very low preheated oven until tender and the meat pulls away from the bone without much resistance. This will take anywhere from 2–4 hours, so be patient!

When cool enough to handle, pick the meat from the bones, discarding the fat if you prefer. Drain the stock, discarding the vegetables, but keep the orange zest, which is now soft enough to eat. Bring the stock up to the boil and reduce by half. Reserve.

Serve the meat reheated in the sauce with the cooked orange zest.

thinly sliced pork, meat juices and tuna dressing

This dish has been adapted from the traditional vitello tonnato, *poached veal with tuna sauce. When we were left with half a roast loin of pork from evening service in the restaurant, we found it made a delicious light lunch when served the following day with either the reheated meat juices, some shaved Parmesan and a few salad leaves, or with this tuna dressing. The important thing here is to serve the meat at room temperature and to slice it incredibly thinly.*

serves 1–2, depending on quantity of pork (the sauce will keep for a few days)

leftover cooked pork loin, shoulder or leg, bone removed

1 tbsp baby capers

salad leaves

Meat juices

a small pan of the meat cooking stock

1 tbsp Dijon mustard

1 garlic clove, peeled and crushed

1 splash of sherry vinegar

a few thyme leaves

1 splash of extra virgin olive oil

salt and pepper

Tuna dressing

2 medium egg yolks

1 small can tuna fillet in oil, drained

1 anchovy fillet

½ garlic clove, peeled and crushed

200ml extra virgin olive oil/salad oil (mix half and half)

1 squeeze of lemon juice

milk

To make the meat juices, bring the reserved meat stock to the boil in a saucepan, then whisk in the Dijon mustard, garlic, sherry vinegar, thyme leaves and olive oil. Taste and adjust the seasoning as necessary. Reserve somewhere warm.

To make the tuna dressing, blend the egg yolks, tuna, anchovy and garlic to a paste in a food processor. Slowly add the olive and salad oils in a thin stream until all is emulsified. Add a squeeze of lemon juice to taste. Let the dressing down with some milk to make a thin consistency. To assemble the dish, slice the pork very, very thinly and layer over a large platter. Simply dress the meat with the juices and tuna dressing. Scatter the baby capers and a few good salad leaves over the top. Serve.

roast duck with foie gras, apples and rosemary

The key to really great crispy duck skin is to lose some of the surplus fat just under the skin and then dry out the duck really well. The skin should become like parchment and the flesh beneath stays beautifully moist.

serves 2 hungry people or 4 supermodels!

1 large duck, rinsed (approx. 2kg)
salt and pepper
1 lobe of foie gras, about 250g in weight
1 large Bramley apple, left whole
1 twig of bay leaves
2–3 sprigs of fresh rosemary
olive oil

Prick the duck all over just under the skin. Start by plunging your whole duck into a saucepan of boiling water: leave for a few minutes then carefully remove from the pan. Leave to dry in a cool place (in front of an open window or an electric fan is ideal) for a few hours. This is quite a laborious process but yields good results. If you really can't be bothered, the dish will still taste as good but the skin won't be so crispy.

Preheat the oven to 220°C/425°F/gas mark 7.

When the duck is very dry, season the cavity and stuff it with the foie gras, then the apple and finally the herbs. Season the bird all over, rub lightly with some olive oil and transfer to a roasting tin. Put it into the hot preheated oven for 15 minutes to blast the skin into crisping up.

After this time turn the oven down and cook slightly slower at about 180°C/350°F/gas mark 4 for another hour. Check the bird after this time and baste with the foie gras and apple juices. It may need a little longer, depending on the oven; if so put it back in for another 10–15 minutes and check after this time. Once out, allow the bird to rest fully for 20 minutes, catching any juices that run out.

These deliciously fatty, flavoursome juices will be your gravy. This is an incredibly rich dish and requires nothing more than simple roast potatoes and maybe a mustard-dressed green salad.

roast woodcock

Woodcock is one of the most prized game birds. They are notoriously difficult to shoot, because of their perfectly camouflaged feathers and their style of flight, twisting and turning over and around trees and hedges. Woodcock have the most beautifully flavoured flesh and, I think, should be handled with great respect and served in the traditional manner.

per person	**1 woodcock, guts left in the bird, trussed in the traditional way with the beak, legs and body tied together (ask your butcher to do this), and rinsed**
	1 bay leaf
	1 sprig of fresh thyme
	2 garlic cloves, peeled
	salt and pepper
	a little olive oil
	25g butter
	a few strips of salted pork fat (or lardo) or streaky bacon rashers
	1 splash of port or Madeira
	1 slice of stale farmhouse loaf, cut on the angle

Preheat the oven to 200–220°C/400–425°F/gas mark 6.

Check the bird over for any stray feathers or loose shot. Stuff the herbs and 1 garlic clove in the cavity (still possible to do, despite the guts being inside) and spear the bird with its own beak. Season with salt and pepper.

In a hot pan seal the bird all over in a little olive oil, ensuring a good golden colour on the breasts. When done smear the butter over the bird, lay the pork fat or bacon over it and put into a roasting tin.

Roast for 10–12 minutes in the hot preheated oven for pink flesh – the only way to eat woodcock. Remove from the oven and place on the hob. Deglaze the tin with the bird still in it using a splash of the booze, then allow the bird to rest for 5 minutes.

Toast or deep-fry the bread. Rub the toast with the remaining raw garlic clove. Now the good bit: tip the bird up, beak upwards, and with a spoon remove the guts from the bird. Spread these on the toast, mashing them a little to ensure even cooking, and put under a hot grill for a few minutes to cook.

When done sit the bird on the toast and tip the resting juices over. Serve with a big bowl of buttered kale or black cabbage and some simple starch, either mustard celeriac or roasted potatoes.

Note: For the more adventurous, take a sharp knife and slice the head and beak in half lengthways exposing the brain (*see* opposite) – this is what the real foodies want to see and eat; in fact, the idea is to use the beak to eat the brain – but this is not one for the faint-hearted.

poached pheasant with gin-soaked muscat grapes

This makes an ideal winter starter or a light main course. It needs some forward planning to marinate the grapes – but you could make a batch and use them in other dishes.

Serves 2 comfortably

2 pheasant breasts
500ml game or chicken stock (*see* page 296)
2 packets baby spinach
olive oil

Gin-soaked grapes
350ml water
330g caster sugar
1kg black seedless Muscat grapes
1 sprig of fresh thyme
1 bay leaf
a few juniper berries
40ml good gin

Boil the water and sugar together in a saucepan to melt the sugar. Remove and cool.

Wash the grapes and put them in a container with the aromatics. Add the gin and enough of the sugar syrup to cover. Store for a few weeks.

In a saucepan, poach the pheasant breast until medium rare in a light game or chicken stock for no longer than 6–8 minutes. Do not allow to boil, then allow to rest.

Toss some baby spinach in some olive oil and poaching liquor over a medium heat for about 1 minute.

Slice the pheasant breast on a serving plate with some spinach and spoon the grapes soaked in gin over the pheasant.

opposite *Steve Roberts, the local art teacher, supplies my restaurant with game throughout the season. He is an exceptional shot. Here he is with his gundogs and a rather nervous-looking Henry!*

mixed seafood stew with spicy mayonnaise

We served this at Alastair Little's restaurant every day for over two years. It is still one of my most enjoyable dishes to prepare and serve, and is great to put in the middle of the table and let everyone dig in. It is fine to use a selection of seafood or just one fish.

serves 4

**about 800g fish: say 100g thick
white fish fillets, 2 scallops
each, 1 handful of mussels and
80g brown shrimps, rinsed
seasoned plain flour
olive oil
croûtons, to serve**

Fish stock
**olive oil
2 celery sticks, sliced
2 carrots, diced
1 white onion, peeled and diced
1 garlic bulb, smashed up
1 star anise
1 red chilli
1 small bunch of fresh thyme**

**a few fresh tarragon stalks
bay leaves
about 2kg fish trimmings, from good
white fish (no eyes, gills or oily fish),
and crab, lobster and prawn shells
are particularly good, all rinsed
1 tbsp tomato purée
125ml Noilly Prat
water, to cover**

Spicy mayonnaise
**1 recipe for basic mayonnaise (*see*
tartare sauce on page 85)
2 or 3 anchovies, mashed
1 dried red chilli, crushed
1 small pinch of saffron strands
a few drops of Tabasco sauce**

Heat a film of oil in a large frying pan and throw in the celery, carrot and onion. Sweat for 10 minutes or so. If using shellfish, tap each shell with a knife, discarding any that do not close. Add the aromatics and stir in the fish bits. Continue stirring erratically for 5–10 minutes. Remove and discard any shellfish that do not open. Add the tomato purée and cook out for a further 2 minutes, then add the Noilly Prat. Boil the alcohol for a few minutes. Cover the fish pieces with water and simmer for 45 minutes, stirring occasionally to avoid the fish bones sticking to the bottom of the pan. Pour through a colander and skim off any orangey-looking fat.

For the spicy mayonnaise, stir all the ingredients together in a bowl and rest to allow the flavours to develop. Now lightly dust the fish fillets or chunks in some seasoned flour and fry them off in a little hot oil for 3–4 minutes until golden. Turn them over and then add the scallops. When you have colour on these, turn them over and add a ladle of the stock. Gently simmer to finish the cooking. Now add the shrimps and stir through for a couple of minutes. Do not let the stock boil as the shellfish will toughen.

Put the fish to one side and introduce a large spoonful of spicy mayonnaise. Gently shimmy the pan around to incorporate the mayonnaise and allow the soup to thicken. Serve immediately with some croûtons and some more of the mayonnaise.

salsify in brown butter

It was quite fashionable in Victorian times, but salsify is a bit of a forgotten vegetable now. You could serve this as a starter on its own or to accompany a main course. In my opinion, it goes really well with most fish and I also like to use it like a crudité – to dip into the whole baked stinking bishop (see page 286).

serves 4–6 as a side dish

1kg salsify
lemon juice
salt and black pepper
2 bay leaves
120g butter
1 tsp each of finely chopped fresh chervil and chives
2 tsp finely chopped fresh parsley

Wash the salsify and peel in a bowl of water acidulated with lemon juice until white. Cut into 6–8cm pieces. Place in a saucepan of cold water to cover with some salt and the bay leaves, and bring up to the boil. Simmer until tender, about 10–15 minutes. Allow to cool in the liquid.

Heat the butter in a frying pan until foaming. Add the salsify and toss with the mixed herbs for a few minutes to coat it with butter and herbs.

braised red cabbage

This is a great seasonal staple. I often serve it with venison or some rare roast beef.
I'd avoid anything fishy, though...

serves 4–6 as a side dish

       3 large white onions, peeled and thinly sliced
       50g butter
       50ml extra virgin olive oil
       salt and pepper
       3 large Bramley apples, cored and cut into chunks
       2 sprigs of fresh rosemary
       1 large red cabbage, cored and sliced
       90g light brown sugar
       100ml balsamic vinegar

In a large saucepan sweat the onion down in the butter and olive oil. At this point season with salt and pepper but don't allow to colour. Throw in the sliced Bramley apples and rosemary, and stir around to break the apple down. Now add the sliced red cabbage. This will almost certainly fill the whole pan but don't panic. After a few minutes of vigorously stirring, the quantity will start to reduce.

Cover the pan with a heavy lid to stop the steam from escaping and turn the heat down low. The cabbage will now take anywhere between 45 minutes to 1 hour. Check every now and then, and give it a stir. Don't let the cabbage stick and burn; if it starts to, then add a splash of water.

When the cabbage has broken down, stir in the sugar and caramelize for a few minutes, then add the vinegar and reduce until it has all gone. It won't take long. Taste and serve.

overleaf *Mushroom foraging is as much about getting out for a good walk as it is about actually finding any mushrooms. The woods surrounding us at this time of year are particularly beautiful. Here we found some scarlett meadow wax mushrooms, which look deadly to my mind, but were in fact delicious. I'd always recommend foraging with an expert as it can be a highly uncertain business!*

foil-baked ceps

Use the best-looking ceps you've picked, as they will be the sole focus of the dish. Mop up the juices with plenty of fresh bread or soft polenta and grated Parmesan.

serves 2

150–200g fresh ceps
2–3 bay leaves
2–3 sprigs of fresh thyme
sea salt flakes and black pepper
50ml olive oil
1 garlic clove, peeled and finely sliced
finely grated zest of 1 lemon

Preheat the oven to 200–220°C/400–425°F/gas mark 6–7.

Brush the ceps, but do not wash. Put in a foil square with the rest of the ingredients. Seal up the parcel and bake in a shallow pan of water (to prevent scorching) in the hot preheated oven for 20 minutes or so.

Serve immediately. The ceps should be just soft and giving.

butterscotch pudding
with whisky sauce

*I've used walnuts and prunes in this one. If this is not your thing, just leave them out.
The whisky sauce, however, is essential to the decadence of the dish. Serve with lots
of thick double cream.*

serves 6–8

50g unsalted butter
60g light brown sugar
1 vanilla pod, split and scraped
2 tsp baking powder
225g self-raising flour
1 pinch of bicarbonate of soda
2 medium eggs
300ml milk, warmed
50g shelled walnuts, chopped
50g stoned prunes, chopped

Whisky sauce
85g butter
85g muscovado sugar
200ml double cream
whisky, to taste

Preheat the oven to 180°C/350°F/gas mark 4. Grease a 20cm square baking tin.

Beat the butter, sugar and vanilla seeds together in a bowl. In another bowl, mix the
baking powder with the flour and bicarbonate. Beat the eggs in a third bowl. Slowly
and alternately add small amounts of flour and egg to the butter mixture until all is
incorporated. Do not over-beat the flour as this will toughen the gluten and produce
a dense cake. Add the milk to form a sloppy batter. Stir in the fruits and nuts.

Pour the mix into the baking tin and cook in the preheated oven for 30–40 minutes
until firm.

To make the sauce, boil the butter and sugar together for 5 minutes. Pour in the cream,
bring back to the boil, then add a capful of whisky or two to taste.

Cut out wedges of the sponge pud and coat liberally with the sauce.

spiced bread and butter pudding

Serve simply, good and warm, with clotted cream or, if possible, some home-made custard with chopped-up Seville orange marmalade through it (see pages 289 and 59).

serves 6–8

300ml milk
300ml double cream
1 pinch of salt
1 pinch each of ground cloves and cinnamon
2 vanilla pods, split lengthways
1 drop of almond extract or 50g toasted almonds
5 medium eggs
45g caster sugar
1 handful each of mixed diced fruit and candied peel
4–6 croissants
250g unsalted butter

In a saucepan, infuse the milk, cream, salt, ground spices, vanilla and either the almond extract or toasted almonds over a very gentle heat for 30 minutes. Strain.

Whisk the eggs and sugar together in a bowl then pour in the strained milk and cream mix. Stir and pour through a sieve. Reserve.

Generously scatter the mixed peel and diced fruit into a deep 25 x 35cm ovenproof dish. Cut the croissants in half horizontally. Melt the butter and generously butter the croissants. Lay them in the dish, gently overlapping.

Now pour the custard mix over the top and fill to the top of the dish. There should be almost three times as much custard as bread when finished. You might not get all the custard in. Leave the pudding to stand for 30 minutes to absorb the liquid.

Preheat the oven to 150°C/300°F/gas mark 2.

Pour the remaining custard into the pudding and press the croissants down with your hands to help cover them completely. They will bob around on top – this is fine. Cook in the preheated oven for 30 minutes or so until the pudding is firm with still a little give in the middle.

Turn the oven off and allow to rest with the door ajar. Serve warm.

poached pear with honeycomb and blue cheese

The key thing here is the quality of the honeycomb and the blue cheese – get it right and they make a sublime combination.

serves 4

4 Conference pears
pared zest and juice of 2 lemons
150ml white wine
150ml water
85g caster sugar
2 cinnamon sticks
1 generous pinch of saffron strands
1 tbsp runny honey
about 120g honeycomb and 400g blue cheese, to serve

Peel the pears. Mix the remaining ingredients except the honeycomb and blue cheese together in a suitably sized saucepan and bring to the boil. Add the pears and simmer for 20–30 minutes, depending on the ripeness of the fruit. Chill the pears in the cooking liquor.

Remove the pears, and serve them with a chunk of gooey honeycomb and a thick slice of good-quality, room-temperature blue cheese.

coffee cake, mascarpone and vanilla cream

My mother makes this cake for me every year around Christmas time and over the years it has become my all-time favourite. It is a bit tiramisu-like but simpler to prepare. I think it's utterly delicious and why it's been confined to an outing once a year, I have no idea!

serves 8–10

170g butter
350g caster sugar
3 large eggs, beaten
6 tbsp self-raising flour
500ml water
5 tbsp coffee essence or good-quality strong coffee
5 tbsp brandy

Mascarpone and vanilla cream
250g mascarpone cheese
1 medium egg yolk
1–2 tbsp icing sugar, to taste
1 vanilla pod, split lengthways and scraped
125g crème fraîche

Preheat the oven to 170°C/325°F/gas mark 3. Grease a 30cm springform cake tin.

For the cake, cream the butter and 175g of the sugar together in a bowl until pale. Gradually add the beaten eggs to the butter mix. Carefully fold in the flour, then spoon the mixture into the prepared tin. Bake in the preheated oven for 45–50 minutes. Remove and cool for a while, still in the tin.

Meanwhile, heat together the water, remaining sugar, coffee essence and brandy, just until the sugar has dissolved. When the cake is still warm, prick it all over with a skewer or fork to better absorb the coffee and brandy mixture that you spoon over the top.

Just before serving, make the mascarpone cream. Mix the mascarpone with the egg yolk and icing sugar. Stir in the vanilla seeds and crème fraîche.

Remove the cake from its tin. Serve the soaked cake warm, in slices, with the mascarpone and vanilla cream.

chestnut ice cream

You will need to find sweet chestnut purée for this ice cream. Try your local deli.

serves 6–8

175ml soured cream
175ml double cream
a pinch of salt
a pinch of ground cinnamon
1 vanilla pod, split
4 medium egg yolks
255g can sweet chestnut purée
a pinch of caster sugar (optional)
biscuits, to serve

Chocolate sauce
250ml double cream
150ml milk
270g caster sugar
225g good dark chocolate, broken into pieces
60g butter

For the ice cream, bring both of the creams to the boil in a saucepan with the salt, cinnamon and vanilla pod. Pour over the egg yolks in a bowl. Return to the pan and stir gently over a moderate heat until thickened. Remove from the heat and strain into a bowl.

Stir in the chestnut purée, taste and add a pinch or more of sugar, if using. Churn or freeze.

For the chocolate sauce, boil the cream, milk and sugar in a saucepan until yellow. Add the chocolate and butter, and stir together until melted.

Serve the ice cream with some good biscuits on a pool of chocolate sauce.

whole baked stinking bishop

Traditionally you would bake one of the famous Alpine cheeses like Vacherin, but Stinking Bishop is perfect for the job and so full of flavour, there's no need to look further afield.

serves 2

1 small whole Stinking Bishop cheese in its box
a few sprigs of fresh rosemary or thyme
3–4 chicons of chicory

Preheat the oven to 200°C/400°F/gas mark 6.

Stud the whole cheese in its box with rosemary or thyme, then bake on a baking sheet in the preheated oven for 20 minutes until soft and bubbling.

Serve the chicory as a salad to lighten the load or, along with some roasted salsify (*see* page 270), for dipping into the molten cheese.

espresso and walnut brownie

This is one of the most popular puds on the menu at the restaurant. It is important here to not overcook the brownie. Keeping it slightly molten ensures a delicious texture. Omit the walnuts if so desired.

serves 8–10 generously

170g unsalted butter

200g shelled walnuts, toasted and chopped

300g good dark chocolate, broken into pieces

150g soft brown sugar

4 medium eggs

100g raisins, softened in hot espresso coffee (a double espresso)

150g mascarpone cheese

1 shot of espresso coffee or strong filter coffee

Preheat the oven to 150°C/300°F/gas mark 2.

Melt 20g of the butter and use to line a 30cm cake tin or suitable dish. Grind a handful of the walnuts and put them in the tin too, sticking to the butter. This prevents the cake from sticking.

Melt the chocolate in a bowl over a saucepan of simmering water. In a food processor, blend the butter and sugar until pale. Slowly add each egg, alternating with the raisins and walnuts. At this point the mix will look like it's horribly split, but don't panic because it will all come together when the chocolate is added. Beat in the mascarpone and coffee shot. Finally add the chocolate. Fold together.

Pour into the lined tin and bake in the preheated oven for about 25–30 minutes or until a crack appears round the inside surface. Allow to cool to room temperature.

Serve with maple syrup ice cream (*see* page 288).

maple syrup ice cream

The perfect accompaniment for the espresso and walnut brownie. Make sure you use a good-quality syrup as many 'maple-flavoured syrups' are imitations: these are less expensive than the real stuff, and they usually have little or no real maple syrup content.

serves 8–10 (with the brownie)

300ml good maple syrup
300ml milk
1 vanilla pod, split lengthways
5 medium egg yolks
450ml double cream

Put the maple syrup in a saucepan and reduce by half. In another saucepan, heat the milk and vanilla pod, bringing them to the boil three times to infuse. In a bowl, whisk the yolks until light and pale.

Pour the hot strained milk over the yolks, mix and pour back into a clean pan. Thicken on a gentle heat until the custard coats the back of a spoon. Immediately pour in the double cream and reduced maple syrup.

Sieve and churn in an ice-cream machine, or freeze in a suitable container. This ice cream will never set completely: due to the extremely high sugar content, it will always remain quite molten.

thick custard

This is more akin to the traditional custard I grew up on as a child. Despite years of the more wishy-washy French crème anglaise in restaurants, I still prefer this richer, thicker variety.

makes about 500ml

250ml milk

250ml double cream

2 vanilla pods, split lengthways

8 medium egg yolks

100g light brown sugar

3 tbsp cornflour, slaked with a little water

In a saucepan, boil the milk with the cream and the vanilla.

Beat together the yolks and the sugar in a bowl. Add the cornflour and water to the yolks. Pour the hot milk and cream mixture on to the yolks, and stir. Cook gently, stirring constantly, for 5–10 minutes to make sure you've killed off any floury taste. The thickening will happen quite quickly but the floury taste will take a bit longer to lose. (Make sure the custard doesn't catch at this stage or it will acquire an unpleasant, smoky taste.)

Serve hot with a traditional British sponge pudding or baked seasonal fruits.

chocolate pots with orange shortbread

These are great if you want an easy pudding to prepare in advance of a meal and very minimal effort when ready to serve.

fills about 8 x 150ml pots or small coffee cups

900g good-quality dark chocolate, at least 70% cocoa solids

1.4 litres double cream

450ml milk

200g icing sugar

8 medium egg yolks, very fresh, preferably free-range organic

whipped double cream, cocoa powder and orange shortbread, to serve

Break the chocolate into pieces and put in a bowl. Boil the cream in a saucepan and pour over the broken-up chocolate. Stir to melt. Combine the milk, icing sugar and egg yolks in another bowl. Pour the chocolate mix into the yolks. Stir and combine, then sieve out any egg threads. Strain into suitable pots or coffee cups and allow to set in the fridge overnight.

Serve with some whipped double cream on top, a sprinkling of cocoa powder and the orange shortbread.

orange shortbread

This also works well with some finely chopped crystallized ginger folded into the flour.

makes 50–60 biscuits

120g salted butter

60g caster sugar

finely grated zest of 3 oranges

120g plain flour

60g polenta flour

Beat the butter and sugar together in a bowl until pale. Stir in the orange zest. Fold in the flours and stop when the mix comes together. On a floured surface, roll the shortbread out to 2.5cm thick and chill in rectangular flat packs in the fridge for 30 minutes. Preheat the oven to 160°C/325°F/gas mark 3. Remove from the fridge, roll the shortbread out to 0.5cm thick, cut to the desired shape and dust with more caster sugar. Put on to a baking sheet and cook for 15–20 minutes in the preheated oven until very pale with a slightly golden edge. Remove, cool and serve with the chocolate pots.

amaretti biscuits

These biscuits are the chewy variety of amaretti and keep well for several days in an airtight box.

makes 50–60 biscuits

4 medium egg whites, very fresh
560g icing sugar, plus extra for dusting
1 pinch of salt
1 tsp almond essence
450g ground almonds
1 handful of flaked almonds

Preheat the oven to 150°C/300°F/gas mark 2.

Put 2 of the egg whites into a food processor with half the sugar. Mix with the blade attachment not the whisk – you don't want to fill the biscuits with too much air. Add a pinch of salt, the almond essence, the ground almonds, the remainder of the sugar and egg whites. The consistency should be thick enough to roll.

Dust a work surface with icing sugar and roll out the dough. Roll it up into a sausage of about 1cm in width. Cut the roll into individual 2.5cm pieces and flatten them lightly on a greased baking sheet. Add the flaked almonds, sticking them randomly on the top.

Cook in the preheated oven for 25–30 minutes until the biscuits are firm and can be removed from the sheet easily. The biscuits should be lightly golden in colour. Dust with more icing sugar and serve warm.

BASICS

white fish stock

Use only white fish bones, not oily, such as salmon or mackerel, for fish stock. Veal or beef stock can be made in the same way, with the same quantity of relevant bones, but with a much longer cooking time. On the whole, beef or veal stock should be cooked for no less than 8 hours. The veal bones could be roasted (as in the lamb stock recipe, opposite) to make a dark as opposed to a light veal stock.

makes about 2 litres

> 3kg white fish bones
>
> 2 leeks, cleaned and diced
>
> 2 white onions, peeled and diced
>
> 1 fennel bulb, roughly sliced
>
> 1 garlic bulb
>
> 3–4 bay leaves
>
> 1 head of celery, diced
>
> 1 handful of parsley stalks

Wash the bones, cover with water in a large saucepan and bring to the boil. Skim off any impurities and fat, then top up with more cold water. Add the vegetables and aromatics: the water should cover everything. Bring to the boil, skim once more, then simmer, uncovered, for 20–30 minutes, but no more.

Sieve and store in the fridge or freezer. (Fish stock kept in a fridge will keep for no longer than two to three days.)

lamb stock

makes about 2 litres

3kg lamb bones
1 head of celery, halved
2 white onions, peeled and halved
3 carrots, halved
2 leeks, cleaned and halved
2 garlic bulbs, halved
100ml vegetable oil
1 tbsp tomato purée
1 tsp black peppercorns
2 sprigs of rosemary
3–4 bay leaves

Preheat the oven to 180°C/350°F/gas mark 4.

Brown the lamb bones in a roasting tin in the hot oven until golden brown. This will take 30–40 minutes.

In a large saucepan, sauté the veg in the oil until browned, about 25–30 minutes. Stir in the tomato purée and cook for 5 minutes. Add the lamb bones and aromatics.

Add enough cold water to cover everything and bring to the boil. Skim off the impurities and fat. Reduce the heat and simmer, uncovered, for about 2 hours.

Put through a sieve and refrigerate until needed. The stock will keep for a week in a fridge and a few months in a freezer.

chicken stock

You could make a duck or guinea fowl stock in exactly the same way.

makes about 2 litres

3.5kg chicken carcasses, and wings if possible
1 head of celery, halved
2 white onions, peeled and halved
3 carrots, halved
2 leeks, cleaned and halved
2 garlic bulbs, halved
3–4 bay leaves
½ bunch of fresh thyme
1 tsp black peppercorns

Put the bones, on their own, into a large saucepan. Add enough cold water to cover the bones and bring to the boil. Skim off all the impurities that rise to the surface. Replace the removed water with more cold water. Bring this back to the boil and skim again.

Now add the veg and aromatics, and bring back to the boil. Reduce the heat and simmer, uncovered, for about 3 hours, skimming occasionally.

Pass through a fine sieve and refrigerate or freeze. This will keep in the fridge for a week and in the freezer for many months.

vegetable stock

makes about 1.4 litres

2 white onions, peeled and quartered

2 fennel bulbs

2 leeks

1 head of celery

parsley stalks

1 garlic bulb, cut in half

1 tsp white peppercorns

1 tsp coriander seeds

a few sprigs of aromatic herbs, such as tarragon or chervil

a few bay leaves

1.5 litres cold water

Put all the ingredients into a large saucepan, and bring to the boil. Skim and simmer at the merest blip for about 25 minutes. Strain and cool.

Store in the fridge for no more than a day to ensure its freshness.

mashed potato

serves 4 generously

8 large Maris Piper potatoes, peeled and quartered

salt, to taste

3 bay leaves

100g unsalted butter

200ml double cream

Rinse the potatoes of their starch under running water, or in several changes of water, for about 5 minutes.

Put into a large saucepan and cover with cold water. Add the salt and the bay leaves. Bring to the boil and simmer until tender, which will take up to 30 minutes.

Remove the potatoes from the water. Discard the bay leaves and steam-dry for 5 minutes.

In a clean saucepan bring the butter and cream to the boil, then put to one side. Push the potatoes through a sieve and stir in the hot cream. Serve immediately.

ACKNOWLEDGEMENTS

This book wouldn't have been realised without the dedication and persistence of my wife Lisa and my commissioning editor Becca Spry. Lisa, without your support, encouragement and constant badgering it would never have got off the ground. Becca, your faith in me has turned a mediocre English student into an author…brilliant!

To Chris Terry, your photography is awe inspiring. You've set this book alight. I hope we'll work together soon, preferably somewhere tropical!

To the Mitchell Beazley team, Fiona, Tim, Miranda, Sarah, Susan et al., your professionalism and dedication to the cause is unparalleled. You make me look really good!

A special thank you must go to my fairy godmother – Diana Henry – who started the ball rolling, a true friend indeed.

To Rich and Cath, thank you for loaning us your beautiful house. Rich you are the best sous chef I never had, but don't give up the day job, medicine's more lucrative than cooking.

Thanks to Raoul, Steve Gill, Steve Roberts, Trealy Farm and all the great suppliers who make it easy for me to write menus.

To John and all the loyal staff at The Foxhunter, thank you for supporting me during my absence – you've done yourselves and the restaurant proud, but as John always says, 'Don't thank me, just pay me!' And Sam, my front of house, PA-come-punch bag, thank you for coping with my bad spelling and typing my illegible sentences.

For Mum, Dad and all my family, thank you for encouraging me and nurturing my love of food at such a young age, it's finally starting to pay dividends!

And lastly – but never least – to Lisa, Jessie and Henry, without you none of this would be worth doing. It's all for you.

INDEX